Understanding the Moment

FOCUS ON THE NOW AND GET THE MOST OUT OF YOUR FUTURE

MIGUEL FERNANDEZ

Fulton Books
Meadville, PA

Published by Fulton Books 2024

ISBN 979-8-88982-903-4 (paperback)
ISBN 979-8-88982-904-1 (digital)

Printed in the United States of America

CONTENTS

ACKNOWLEDGMENTS

There are many people I need to thank who have influenced and contributed to this book and the journey that it was to write.

To my father, Angel, you have always been my rock and foundation; and upon your shoulders, I have built my world. To my mother, Ruth, you always challenged me to succeed and loved me when I failed, then picked me up and sent me forward. I miss you. To my wife, Romelia, and my daughters, Eli and Ruthie, you are my inspiration for this book and those that come after it. And finally my sister, Nancy, my voice of conscience, thank you for helping to raise me while our mother was resting in heaven.

To all of those whom I have not mentioned who have contributed to this book in all stages and ways, I thank you, and may you all be blessed.

Introduction

The purpose of life is to go on a journey to become more self-aware and to create one's own identity. "Know thyself" refers to the ability to understand your true nature, expand your consciousness, and grow as a person. This is a birthright. Your request for information will be accepted. If you are experiencing a sense of denial, you have somehow denied yourself, which has caused your perception of time to be stretched. You always have the option to ignore what occurs and continue to understand the world the same way you did the day before. Alternatively, you can be open to new possibilities that provide you with a different reality for today. No matter what happens, life will continue to provide you with an endless stream of information that will help you on your quest. This very second, along with this book, is one of them.

One of the most perplexing questions that humankind has ever tried to answer is where life came from and what its purpose is. Since the beginning of human consciousness, we have endeavored to understand what our lives are all about and why we are here. Many great thinkers, including saints, sages, mystics, philosophers, historians, and poets, have spent their lives trying to find answers to problems as fundamental as "why are we here?" Who or what is responsible for our creation? What are we here to accomplish? Why do we suffer? Why are some people born into this world with good fortune while others appear destined for a life filled with sorrow and misery? Where are we headed, and why? What are the steps that need to be taken to find inner calm? Just who am I?

While the answers to all these questions are necessary for developing awareness, the answer to one fundamental question—"Who am I?"—is the key that unlocks the door to find the solutions to all the other questions. A deep and complete comprehension of oneself answers all other inquiries.

This book will show you how to look at who you are and what you are genuinely capable of experiencing in a fresh, innovative, and illuminating new light. Suppose you permit yourself to be open to new information about the reasons why you are the unique individual that you are. In that case, you will start to see and believe in more of the endless possibilities of who you can become during your lifetime. And it is precisely this realization that will make it possible for you to experience an unlimited stream of calm that has always been accessible to you and will continue to be accessible to you as long as you are here on earth because it is within you. After realizing your endless potential, you can make decisions from a state of mind that is more at ease, lucid, and focused. You can create the reality you eventually want to experience, which is the reality of your dreams, when you are in a solid mental state.

A new perspective on how you identify yourself and how that definition guides you as you create and experience life will be presented to you in the pages that are about to follow. This trip to an expanded state of awareness can go as far as you desire it to go since it depends on the level of intent you have to get the answers to the specific questions you have about life. This journey can go as far as you desire it to go. This information has been brought to your attention because of you. As the person who wrote it, my only responsibilities have been to organize and present it. You have an opportunity in this now, as you do in every moment, to determine whether or not you are prepared to experience more of who you are.

This book walks the reader through, step by step, the process that goes into the making of "You." Constructing a framework before transmitting the following information is necessary to do so successfully. As a result, the book is divided into three distinct parts that cover a wide range of topics. Each subsequent section offers information crucial to the broader process of coming to terms with one's identity, building on the foundation laid by the parts that came before it. If you need to understand a topic, you must review a previous section to get a better grasp before moving on.

PART 1

WHO ARE YOU?

A Deeper Understanding of Who You Are

In this life, we are surrounded by chaos. It is in everything and always seeking to distract us from the true purpose of what we are to become. You may be asking me what that is, and the answer is simple—*more*. As a race (human), we are given many abilities above the other inhabitants and animals of this world. Humans, more than any other species, have enormous potential. How do we maximize that potential? That is the real purpose of the book.

So How Do We Maximize Potential?

Before you can maximize your potential, you must understand who you are. It is challenging to understand who you are because, as I said before, chaos continuously encircles our perception of who we see ourselves to be.

When I was younger, I defined myself by what I did. As a young hotshot chiropractor, I thought all I had to do was hang a shingle with my name on it, and patients would pour through my door and make me a rich chiropractor. I was wrong. I struggled; my business struggled. Even though I was a good chiropractor and my patients always got better, I needed to understand why the office did not see the volume needed to succeed.

I looked for the reason outside the practice. But the cause was not out there. The problem was internal. I did not believe in myself on the subconscious level. I had habits (procrastination and laziness) that could be better when growing a business. I also had a fear of my own, a fear of taking risks, a fear of the unknown, and a fear that I could not make something, especially a business, succeed.

CHAPTER 1

You Are Matter and Energy

*M*atter can be defined as anything that takes up space and can be experienced by one or more of the five senses that make up the human body. As a result, you are a singular constituent of the material world. It needs a certain amount of power for matter to inhabit space. The force responsible for your existence as matter is the same force that generates and maintains every other particle of matter in the universe: energy. There is no*thing* other than energy that lies behind any*thing* that exists.

It takes a certain amount of force and the intention for anything to remain in the state of matter for energy to be able to do so. Therefore, the driving force behind all creation is an intention, also known as the will to exist. This force transforms an endless amount of energy into a finite form of matter. The wave of potentiality, which represents energy, is bound into the particle, meaning matter, so that it may be detected. Everything observed in the world has a "will" to express itself. The "will" is apparent in the intention of the atoms that form the molecules that produce the form that any particular piece of matter has taken in the universe. These molecules are responsible for producing the form that any specific amount of matter has taken.

Every single item in the universe, from a mineral to a plant to an animal to a human being, constantly communicates the purpose for which it was created. Try cracking a boulder or rock in half with your own hands if you don't believe it has any kind of will. It has been discovered that intention is the single most potent and creative force known to mankind. This concept of the unending cycle of the transformation of energy into matter is expressed by the well-known formula developed by Einstein, which is known as $E = mc^2$ (energy equals mass times the speed of light squared).

Stars, planets, entire solar systems, and galaxies have all been generated by a constant force of energy into matter. This force was paired to build matter into a limitless number of structures, systems, and patterns throughout the universe. There is no other form just like any of these. When we look around the world we live in, we can see that it is teeming with an infinite number of unique "things." Each of these "things" that exist in our world has been through its own amazing and accumulative journey, which has sculpted it into the form it is currently expressing. This journey has been passed down from generation to generation. The will to exist is connected with the self-evident goal of each "thing," although no two roads are the same.

One or more distinguishing characteristics can be used to categorize each type of matter in the cosmos. For instance, the fact that there were over 1.8 million different species known to exist on earth as of the most recent census is an impressive demonstration of the currently manifested varied forms of possibility that have developed from an infinitely capable capacity for creation. When viewed from a greater distance, many of these individual things may have a shape and size that is comparable to one another. However, once you observe more carefully and in greater detail, you will notice a growing number of distinctions and variations among the categories of things that initially appeared to be comparable. From a cursory examination, you may conclude that "a beetle is a beetle." However, if you do some additional research, you will discover that, astonishingly, over 350,000 different species of beetles live on our globe.

People frequently appear identical to one another when viewed from a great distance. However, upon closer examination, we are found to have various distinguishing characteristics, the first of which is our outward presentation. We each have a unique facial structure, height, and color of our eyes and hair. We also speak various languages and dialects according to the region where we were raised. Not only are there variances common on separate continents, but distinctions are also prevalent on each continent. For example, people who live in Europe can communicate with one another using nearly two hundred distinct languages. In addition, we can further differentiate ourselves based on our cultural practices, such as the religious observances, culinary preferences, and clothing trends that we adhere to. There are at least as many diverse ways of life, fashions, languages, and dialects in the United States as there are regions in the country. The question "How are you doing?" has a very distinctive tone in the city of Seattle in contrast to the tone it has in Jersey City.

The primary argument is that matter has continuously adapted to its surroundings and developed into various novel forms worldwide. Every form or representation of matter known today is the product of millions of years of activity and reaction between matter and its surrounding environment. The changes that have occurred generation after generation as a result of these activities have occurred because of a singular aim shared by all generations. This continual development takes place in a moment-to-moment basis, with everything in the universe harmonizing with the environment to maintain the experience of existing as it was designed, which is to survive.

This purpose is continually being communicated through nature. Sunlight is an example of an essential factor that contributes to the continued existence of plant life. Because of this, everything, from grass to trees, finds a way to grow in the direction of light to absorb as much energy as possible for the sake of development and survival. The natural ecosystem, which is always in flux, is a superb example of the ongoing struggle to adapt, create harmony, and maintain equilibrium. The ability of many insects and lizards to change color and blend into their current environment to avoid being seen by predators is one example of continuous adaptation. Other examples include the shifting migratory patterns of certain fish due to climate change, the shift in spawning locations for certain fish due to climate change, and the ability of certain birds to change their migration patterns. The process of adaptation in the natural world is hardwired and automatic.

It is clear from seeing how the behaviors of various multicellular organisms evolve throughout the time that the primary goal of life is to maintain its existence. This happens when an organism can successfully harmonize with the environment in which it lives. If an organism cannot discover a means to fit in with its surroundings or adjust to its conditions, it will not be able to continue existing for very long.

When it comes to human beings, once our continued existence in the environment is not in question, social integration and acceptance emerge as the preeminent means by which we can feel pleased and alive. Even as recently as one hundred years ago, most individuals in industrialized nations like the United States spent their days either hunting or fishing to provide for themselves and their families. There were only a few hypermarkets and vast supply chains for construction materials, so getting the things essential for day-to-day life took a lot of work. People in the past felt incredible fulfillment and contentment since they could achieve and experience the fundamental human requirements of food and shelter. However, this changed in the last several hundred years. Except for people living in excellent deprivation conditions, these essential requirements are no longer as much of a concern on a day-to-day basis for people who live in the modern, developed world. Many people today have grown to rely more and more on social acceptance to determine whether they are still alive and whether or not they matter in the world.

The priority of social acceptance can be summed up in the following thought process: If I'm accepted, I'm adored. If I'm liked, I matter. If I am important, then I must exist. Every day, people exhibit their need for social acceptability through cultural views, moral actions, the accumulation of material things, and religious beliefs. This need is so intense that the more a person yearns to be linked to or accepted by others, the more inclined they will be to give up the powerful capacity of independent will or mind and surrender to the behavior and thought of the group. This is because this need is so strong.

When an individual, in response to this urge, represses his or her independent, creative thoughts and ideas, this can result in a wide variety of mental conflicts within the individual. These intense thoughts and sentiments are frequently repressed because people are afraid of being socially marginalized for having beliefs that oppose those held by the group. This capacity for independent thought will also be given up in many religious organizations if a person fears losing approval from some acquired understanding of the concept of God. This is because such anxieties are common. Because of this anxiety, people often may "sell their souls" to have the impression that they are accepted. When applied to this situation, the expression "selling one's soul" refers to relinquishing one's unique capacity for creative and intuitive thought, resulting from having an open and unrestricted mind. People frequently suppress their emotions and ideas to gain the acceptance and approval of other people or to cater to what they have been taught to believe are the wishes and requirements of a higher power.

The tremendous power people have to think for themselves is lost in direct speed and proportion to the degree that people believe they need to "fit in" to feel as though they are accepted and matter. This loss of power occurs in direct speed and proportion to the number of people who believe this. When the pressure to fit in and belong is very intense, situations like this frequently arise in high school, particularly inside certain cliques or street gangs. In addition to these settings, religious organizations, the workplace, and political groupings are also potential breeding grounds for such behavior.

Many well-known examples of this kind of group behavior throughout history illustrate the disastrous results that can occur when there is such a strong need to be accepted and matter in some way. These examples come from different periods, but they all have one thing in common: they come from groups of people. When combined, profound terror and the instinct to survive almost always obliterate any trace of rational cognition. The Holocaust, which Nazi Germany's Third Reich carried out; the mass suicide that took place in the Peoples Temple in Guyana in 1978, which the Reverend Jim Jones led; and the genocide of ethnic Tutsis in Rwanda in 1994, which Hutu extremists carried out, are some of the more extreme examples from recent history. In each of these instances, the dominating element that overrode and stifled the individual's creative personal will and truth was the perceived desire for membership in a group, mixed with the fear of being excluded from the acceptable social norm. This combination was the dominant force.

No one else in the world have followed the same path of decisions that led you to this moment. The course of evolution that each creature has taken is unique, which is the primary reason why there are no two objects in the universe that are completely identical. As a result of the fact that no two snowflakes have ever been found to be identical, this potent form of creativity is frequently expressed whenever it snows. These millions of varied crystallized flakes are falling from above, and as they do so, they are symbolically displaying the magnificence of the limitless creative potential of the universe. If you give any thought to the significance of things like matter and difference, you start to realize and experience the core of creation.

The Relativity of Who You Are

Because we live in a world governed by relativity, we must define who we are to everything else that is made of matter to understand our place in the universe. Our sense of self-definition is something that emerges from an infinite number of dichotomies, such as high and low, big and little, hot and cold, wet and dry, up and down, east and west, loud and quiet, hard and soft, alive and dead, and so on. Everything that exists contributes to our ability to better define ourselves as unique human beings.

As a human being, you define who you are every minute by how you respond in connection to every other "thing" you interact with. This happens every single second. (This pertains to both individuals and events.) Every experience allows you to demonstrate who you are by your reactions to it in several different ways. If you continue along this train of thought, you will one day realize that everything in the cosmos serves a function, which is the ultimate conclusion you will reach. Because everything makes it possible for every other aspect of existence to have an unlimited field of context in which to experience itself through self-expression, everything serves to increase the definition and differentiation of everything else.

Every atom, molecule, and particle in the universe serves a specific function essential to the overall experience matrix. Everything else gains definition and dimension from each object. Because of this diversity, life can experience itself in an infinite variety of contexts through the ways it may express itself. Similarly, everything in your life does so for a specific reason and a purpose that ultimately benefits you.

Your purpose is being fulfilled for everything and everyone whose field of awareness you enter every day and every minute. It is a truth that is spoken by all of creation. You are an essential component of everything in the universe, which is interconnected and dependent on one another for survival. Simply your presence is all that is required to serve this purpose. Your mission as an imaginative and creative human being in this world is not to determine *whether* you will matter but rather *how* you will matter at every stage of the journey. This *how* is the essence of free will, which dwells in everyone, including you.

The less authority you claim to have in the creation of your life, the more readily you can be influenced or will succumb to the creative power and energy of the people around you. This is because you have less control over your own life. If you are not actively constructing your path, other people, including your boss, children, strangers, political and religious leaders, or any other person or object, will choose it for you. The decision that is available to you in every moment of your life is whether or not you are ready to realize more of the power that lies within you to create and gain complete control over your life consciously or whether you will allow your intentions and your creative desires to second to the creative purposes of others. If you are ready to realize more of the power that lies within you to create and gain complete control over your life consciously, then you have the option to make the decision.

Experiences come and go in a never-ending cycle throughout life. If you permit yourself to be open to new, creative experiences and ideas, you will broaden your knowledge of the decisions that can be made for your life. Your progress can be summed up in this new-found insight regarding how you can redefine yourself. The concept of evolution can be boiled down to the new avenues of self-definition that become available as a direct result of increasing one's knowledge.

CHAPTER 2

How You Experience Your Self-Definition

Your beliefs about yourself write the tune of how the rest of your life will go. They define what you believe you can do, both consciously and unconsciously. Your self-worth, much like a hardworking actor, follows the role it's supposed to play perfectly. It is responsible for validating your script and bringing it to "life" by implementing it in the existing environment. Therefore, you can argue that your beliefs are similar to the seeds containing what you wish to "be" daily. Your self-worth is the mechanism—an automatic process that arises from inside you—that drives the activities you take to nurture these seeds into whole experience and realization. These attempts are driven by your desire to bring these seeds into the whole experience and fruition.

Your self-worth will resort to any method of interpretation of the external world that it deems essential to confirm your views. Self-worth does not care if you are in harmony with the reality of what is taking place in your life; it is focused solely on itself. The only thing that matters is whether or not your self-worth has completed the task of validating your self-image through the experience that you have had. For instance, a person can "think" that they are the best husband or wife in the world; nevertheless, until that person actually "experiences" what it is like to be a great husband or wife, their "thoughts" will stay just that, thoughts. The longer it is treated as a theory, the greater the need to have direct experience with the concept will become in establishing confidence in it.

Similarly, a person can "believe" that they are a great athlete, but if they don't get the chance to actually "be" a great athlete, then their belief is open to question. They will, at some point, need to demonstrate their athletic prowess by accomplishing something that substantiates the claim that "I *am* a terrific athlete," which eventually depicts who they are.

People are typically considered *grounded* and *down to earth* when their self-definitions are under the reality of what is happening. They look at ease with who they are and how they express themselves, giving the impression that they are at ease with themselves. They do not care how other people perceive them in any way. Self-worths have little to do with people like these because their self-identity is congruent with the world around them.

People whose self-definitions are not in sync with reality are typically seen as being *out of touch, delusional,* or having an *inflated self-worth*, among other negative connotations. These people consistently give off an edgy vibe and have the propensity to behave awkwardly. Since they cannot relax, getting their attention may be challenging. It looks as though they are constantly surrounded by conflict. Because their perception of who they are is almost always at variance with the evidence in the real world, self-worth is always trying to find a means to divert their attention away from the truth or bring them back into harmony with it.

Your self-worth will battle for whatever belief you have about yourself and will go to any lengths to achieve its aim of self-validation. Your self-worth's goal is to validate itself. It is tasked with only producing the experience of the self-defining assertions of who you are and finally becoming the "I am" that you have stated to bring about the desired state of mind of calm. The only time the self-worth experiences difficulties are when your "I am" contradicts what you have built your self-worth with. Afterward, self-worth goes into overdrive and makes an all-out effort to fix the problem it caused. You can either surrender to the new truth and change the belief in direct conflict with it or you can find a means to entirely reject what is being offered to you, which is the final resolution to the conflict between your self-worth and your self-defining self.

How the Use of Your Self-Worth Allows You to Understand Better Who You Are

Self-worth has been the subject of a great deal of misinterpretation throughout history. On the way to peace, many traditions will tell you that you must either master your self-worth or let it die. The opposite is true. Self-worth is a part of you that is neither a positive nor a negative component of your being. It is merely the part of you that is active and reacts to your circumstances to safeguard the image of yourself that you have created: *I am*. Your self-worth is not something that can be wrestled or fought with. It is not something that needs to be eradicated to achieve a state of contentment and tranquility. Self-worth is merely a concept that has to be understood.

Your self-worth's job is to provide you with a unique experience among all the possibilities in the cosmos. The fact that millions of individuals don't realize that their self-worths are driving them is a problem that has to be addressed. This is not the case at all. The delusion that you are powerless over your circumstances is what is controlling you. This misperception is to blame for the ongoing pain experienced by many individuals. You have complete control over your self-worth at all times. "It shall be as you tell it," the ancient Chinese proverb says. Self-worth will seek to validate whatever you declare yourself to be, from "*I am* depressed and in debt" to "*I am* happy and free" and everything in between.

Suppose your self-worth has difficulties persuading you that you are who you believe you are. In that case, it will use any inventive mental illusions and tricks to make you feel you have been appropriately validated. For this reason, people who constantly need to have their self-worths "stroked" are those who demand frequent reassurance of how amazing they are. When experiencing feelings of insecurity, you are more inclined to seek temporary comfort from various sources "outside" of yourself, such as other people, things you own, or events. This continuous stream of external affirmation would be required to soothe the internal struggle you are experiencing so long as the erroneous idea that is the root cause of your uneasiness is not recognized.

When your self-worth has finally used up all its available illusions, it is obliged to submit to the truth that the present moment presents. This acceptance brings an immediate stop to the struggle and relieves the suffering. A fresh iteration of you comes into being. The effort your self-worth needs to undertake will become less demanding once your "I am" statements ("I am" statements come from the self-defining and self-realization of who you are) fully align with the reality that you are. Your self-worth will only behave in response to a situation in which you feel the need to validate a particular idea about yourself or the world that is either not taking place at this time or is being called into question in some way.

When you hand over the power to validate yourself to other people, you jeopardize your self-worth by not being satisfied in a way that would allow you to keep your composure and stay at peace with yourself. Your self-worth will not conflict with yourself and your environment if other people agree with what your self-worth has registered as who you are. The inner state of the self has not changed. Your self-worth, however, will fly into overdrive if other people tell you that they don't like what you're wearing. There is a discrepancy between who you believe you are and what the world presents as the truth about who you are. In this scenario, the self would be momentarily invalidated, and your bruised self-worth would be required to return to its duties.

CHAPTER 3

How Insecurities Damage Who You Are

A sense of insecurity is something that nearly all people will, at some point in their lives, go through, and this sensation can have many different origins. In most cases, it manifests as a lack of self-assurance, accompanied by uneasiness and doubt. A person can discover renewed security, stability, and a sense of value that propel them toward pleasure and greater well-being if they appropriately recognize and address their feelings of insecurity. This will help limit the negative influence that insecurity has on them.

What Does It Mean to Be Insecure?

Insecurity is characterized by a general apprehension or uncertainty regarding your worth, abilities, skills, and value. This feeling conveys that one is in jeopardy or danger from something or someone. Feeling unsafe can affect one's physical, mental, or emotional health. It is possible to achieve complete trust or perform to the best of your abilities with enough security.

Being insecure means feeling uncertain or lacking confidence in yourself or your abilities. It can manifest in various ways, such as feeling inadequate or unworthy, doubting oneself, or constantly seeking validation from others. Insecurity can stem from various sources, such as past traumas, negative self-perception, or social comparisons. It can also result from external factors, such as criticism or rejection.

Being insecure can affect an individual's mental and emotional well-being, leading to low self-esteem, anxiety, and depression. It can also impact one's behavior and relationships, causing one to shy away from new challenges or to seek constant reassurance from others. Overcoming insecurity often requires a combination of self-reflection, positive self-talk, and seeking support from others. It can be challenging, but addressing and working through insecurity can lead to increased confidence and overall well-being in the future.

Why Do You Have Low Self-Esteem?

Past experiences influence the degree of insecurity a person feels. There is also the possibility of a biological connection, in which insecurity is an inherited trait passed down through the generations and expressed through temperament and personality. Alternatively, an individual may have a mental health condition that contributes to their feelings of insecurity.

Types of Insecurities

Personal insecurity

Insecurities about one's appearance or voice and concerns about how others perceive one are personal insecurities. These surface-level fears, such as fretting about one's hair or wardrobe or being self-conscious about an unpleasant blemish, may appear trivial to an observer looking in from the outside.

However, they may be experienced significantly by the individual and result in unease. If we give in to them, our doubts about ourselves can even prohibit us from seeking romantic relationships, professional chances, or social interactions with other people.

They may originate from worrying too much about what other people think of you, which can lead to a lack of self-confidence. They frequently, but only sometimes, connect to one's body perception.

People who use social media platforms are more likely to compare themselves to others, exacerbating their feelings of insecurity and driving them to develop harmful coping methods, such as eating disorders and self-inflicted injuries.

Professional insecurity

People have professional anxieties at their places of employment, which may make them uneasy and self-conscious when it comes time to give presentations or speak their minds.

People who struggle with these fears may also work with self-doubt, leading them to assume that they are not qualified for promotions or to take risks. It causes people to suffer from the impostor syndrome and prevents them from accomplishing their goals.

Relationship insecurity

Insecurities about one's partner are prevalent and can arise in any relationship. They will make you feel you are not deserving of your spouse and that they would be better with someone else.

These anxieties may result in envy, disputes, and conduct that is dominant over others. Insecurities about relationships can be traced back to a person's past traumatic experiences, whether those experiences were with a former partner or with other friends or family members.

What Causes Insecurities?

To overcome our fears, we must first understand what leads to them and where they originated. Although it may be challenging to identify the precise root of each of our concerns, gaining a deeper comprehension of the factors that contribute to insecurity can assist us in overcoming these feelings and moving on with our lives.

According to the findings of specific studies, how we react to recent experiences in our lives accounts for 40 percent of our overall satisfaction. People's confidence and sense of self-worth can take a hit when they experience setbacks in any area of their lives, whether professional or personal.

Imagine for a moment that your superior at work chose someone else to receive an exceptional promotion that you have worked very hard to earn. This defeat would completely devastate you and have a devastating effect on your sense of self-worth.

If the emotion of failure is not processed and dealt with, it can develop into a more severe inner critic. You can strive for perfectionism because you believe that you will never feel confident or pleased without it.

Insecurity is another effect brought on by social anxiety. People who struggle with self-assurance in social settings, such as family gatherings, professional meetings, job interviews, and first dates, often experience anxiety about how others will evaluate them.

Are they evaluating the quality of my shoes? Is my chuckle coming off as overly loud to them? Have I just made a moronic remark? All these are notions that someone who lacks confidence could have.

Social anxiety can be brought on by adverse events from the past, such as being bullied, having loved ones turn their backs on you, or having other instances of others evaluating you too severely.

When we have had terrible experiences in the past, it can be challenging to accept ourselves and our faults. But if we improve ourselves, we will see an improvement in our confidence.

How to Overcome Insecurity

We can start to combat our insecurity after a greater understanding of where it originates from and its substantial effect on our lives. Once we have this knowledge, we can begin to take action. Let's get started by stopping the practice of listening to our critical inner voice. Dr. Robert Firestone established the cognitive, emotional, and behavioral method known as voice therapy to assist patients in overcoming their critical inner voice. This method can be broken down into five key stages, each of which I will describe in more detail below.

Step 1

The initial phase of voice therapy consists of verbalizing your self-critical ideas while referring to yourself in the third person. You may also write these thoughts down for yourself. Instead of writing "I am so stupid," try "I am so dumb. What could be wrong with me?" You may respond with anything like, "You are so incredibly dim-witted. You will never achieve what you want." This approach allows you to detach yourself from these brutal attacks by framing them as the work of an external foe rather than as an expression of your perspective. Because making these remarks can bring up underlying memories from the past, this process may also be emotionally taxing.

Step 2

In the second stage, you may reflect on and discuss the feelings and insights you've gained from revealing these negative beliefs. Are there people or things from your past that come to mind when you think of them? Discovering the connection between these vocal assaults and the early life circumstances that had a role in molding them may be beneficial in some instances. You will be able to experience some self-compassion and dismiss these attitudes as inaccurate representations of who you are due to this.

Step 3

The third phase of this process is one that many people struggle with since it requires standing up to long-held assumptions and fears about oneself. You will respond to the attacks against your voice by presenting the truth about your position. You have the option of writing down remarks that are logical and truthful about how you truly feel. Respond to your assaults with the same compassion and love you would show to a friend saying similar things about himself or herself.

Step 4

In the fourth phase of voice therapy, you will begin to establish connections between the voice attacks you have been having and the actions you are engaging in. What kind of impact do they have on you at work? With your significant other? As a parent? In terms of your personal goals? Do they bring you down in any way? Which occurrences brought on the feeling of insecurity? In what spheres does this sense of uneasiness have the largest impact?

Step 5

The final step involves making a plan to change these behaviors. If insecurity keeps you from asking someone on a date or going after a promotion, it's time to do the actions anyway. If you're indulging in self-hating thoughts that encourage you to engage in self-destructive behaviors, it's time to interrupt them and unleash the real you.

This process will take work. With change always comes anxiety. These defenses and critical inner voices have been with you your whole life, and they can feel uncomfortable to challenge. When you do change, expect the voices to get louder. Your insecurities aren't likely to vanish overnight, but slowly, through perseverance, they will weaken. Stand up to it whenever you notice an attack and don't indulge in its directives. If you want to be healthy, don't let it lure you into avoiding exercise. If you want to get closer to your partner, don't listen when it tells you to hold back your affections.

How to Live with Insecurities

Insecurities, like other mental illnesses, can be alleviated by adjusting one's way of living and one's point of view. Seeing a therapist can significantly assist you if you have trouble accomplishing these things independently. It takes time and patience to change your routines. Therefore, to experience more permanent effects, you should be willing to keep interventions over a lengthy time.

Consult a mental health professional.

In the same way, you wouldn't try to set your broken bone or remove your gallbladder yourself. You shouldn't resolve your fears alone if they require professional attention. Therapists can deliver the therapy modality that is both the most effective and the most efficient in terms of establishing extended periods of well-being and security.

Although it could appear to be a challenging task, looking for a therapist is pretty straightforward. You can get advice for treatment from a friend, your primary care physician, or your insurance company. You can also call your insurance company. Consider using an online therapist directory that allows you to search based on geography, area of expertise, and types of insurance accepted.

Recognize the impact that uncertainty has on your everyday life.

When you suffer from insecurity, you could have the impression that the issue is just present sometimes or that it does not significantly impact any aspect of your life. These points of view may be accurate, but it is incredibly beneficial to take an honest look at your life and ask yourself how insecurity affects your schoolwork, job, trust in others, communication ability, sense of self-worth, and mental health.

Investigate the cause of the insecurity.

When a person is insecure, they may perceive that circumstances are causing difficulties for others or themselves. Factors from the outside world almost always cause uncertainty, but it is ultimately up to the individual to find a solution. Be sure to create therapies that target the source of the individual's growing sense of insecurity, whether it be past life experiences, mental health difficulties, or current relationships.

Engage in acts of self-compassion that are not conditional.

When dealing with insecurity, you will require significant compassion and self-love daily. You will be able to effect more substantial change in the world if you give these to yourself rather than trying to get them from other people. Loving oneself results in an increased sense of safety and well-being.

Reparent yourself.

Your parents' early teachings and examples contributed to your unease. You can teach yourself new perspectives by closely examining your beliefs about yourself, other people, and the world around you. You may fortify your sense of safety and self-worth by going through this procedure.

Be open and honest about the concerns you have regarding your safety.

Insecurity causes people to be unsure and uncertain about relationships, which leads to them not feeling comfortable enough to share their experiences and feelings with others. However, this approach only breeds isolation and shame because it prevents people from communicating their thoughts and emotions. Your relationship may suffer due to a lack of communication; thus, you should take the opposite approach and be open with trustworthy supporters about what you go through and what they can do to assist you. Make sure that your expectations are in line with reality. Share your insecurity with the people closest to you and your mental and physical health–care providers.

Establish good personal relationships with people.

There will always be a time when you require a powerful group of people. Having loved ones and friends who are in good health and happy around you will help you change your viewpoints even more from the ideas you have held in the past. They can introduce you to new environments, people, and experiences that can help you increase your confidence.

Stay positive.

Your insecurities will significantly influence your internal dialogue with yourself and how you perceive the outside environment. People who talk more positively to themselves, confront their negative self-talk, focus on the future, and look for positive things in their environment tend to be more secure and comfortable in their skin. At first, you may find these principles strange, but in the long run, they will prove beneficial.

Pay attention to your own physical well-being.

Taking care of your mental health and improving your self-esteem can be accomplished by engaging in physical activity, obtaining adequate rest, and eating more healthful meals. It is generally true that when people are healthier physically, they are also healthier mentally; therefore, it is best to begin with tiny improvements and gradually establish consistency through time.

Recognize your boundaries and embrace your uniqueness while doing so.

Alteration is desirable, and people can realize greater levels of success by venturing in novel directions. People get into trouble when they become obsessed with changing things that cannot be changed. Learn to make peace with your insecurities and accept the things you cannot alter. Find strategies to get comfortable with the things that make you uneasy.

Strive for improvement rather than perfection.

It is not feasible to experience complete and utter safety at all times. There is no such state as perfection; therefore, you should strive for advancement. Take a moment to reflect on where you started, where you are, and where you intend to go. Appreciate the route you're on and maintain your dedication to moving forward.

<h1>CHAPTER 4</h1>

How People Shape Who You Are

Growing up, I had many friends who shaped the man I am now. The people who had the most significant impact on my young life were my circle of friends, the environment, and my parents. Friends have a way of challenging one another to be better or have a way of diminishing their potential.

Let us see how the people we keep around us make or break who we are and who we can be.

You may be familiar with the idea put out by Jim Rohn, which states, "You are the average of the five people you spend the most time with."

According to this rule, the five people we spend the most time with influence who we become. The law of averages, which states that "the result of any given scenario will equal the average of all occurrences," is the source of this idea. Therefore, although we maintain connections with a large number of people, the few individuals who are most significant in our lives are the ones who genuinely shape our way of thinking and the choices we make.

Earlier, the famed German author Goethe expressed this idea: "Tell me whom you consort with, and I will tell you who you are." And even earlier than that, Seneca penned the following letter to a friend: "Choose a person whose words, way of life, and face, as a reflection of the character behind it, somehow won your approval.

Maintain a constant focus on him, either as your protector or your model, and do so throughout the day. There is a requirement for someone to serve as a benchmark for our characters so that they can evaluate how they stack up against others. You need a ruler to compare your work to make crooked things straight."

Tony Robbins, a well-known life coach, says that "the quality of a person's life is most frequently a direct reflection of the expectations of their peer group." Therefore, our lives mirror our standards or the things that we are ready to put up with.

Many individuals are willing to put up with bad relationships, miserable occupations, and miserable ways of life. When people of this nature surround us, it significantly impacts who we are, to the point where our talent and "potential" become meaningless. Consequently, a great deal of potential still needs to be realized.

If those who are closest to us have the potential to impact our lives negatively, the question then becomes why we continue to keep them in our lives.

Why Do People Socialize with the Same Group of People Over and Over Again?

Most people choose their friends depending on how close they live to them rather than any other factor. This holds especially true for younger children and adolescents, but it frequently does so even for adults.

Consider your time spent in school as an example. It's improbable that you chose your buddies based on whether or not they shared their interests and characteristics. It was more about who lived in the neighborhood or sat next to you in class than anything else.

Most people can adjust to whatever setting they find themselves in. They have what is known in psychology as an "external locus of control," which means that they believe that their lives are directed by things that are not controlled. As a result, people live their lives in response to the challenges that life presents to them.

Our routines and points of view on the world have been greatly influenced by the people we have spent our lives with, particularly in our formative years. This is especially true of our younger selves. In particular, our mothers had a significant amount of impact on this.

This has significantly impacted who we are, and we ought to be thankful for it. But regardless of how we feel about it or how much we want to change it, nothing can be done about it. We can be pro-active in our quest for people to associate with who can assist us in achieving the goals that we have set for ourselves in life, both now and in the future.

This is made much simpler by developments in technology, the expansion of the Internet, and notably, the proliferation of social media. We can now transition from a local setting to one in which we can connect with groups of people worldwide. One's physical location no longer hinders that.

In addition, there is a mushrooming number of communities of people who have very particular passions and can assist us in achieving happiness, mental tranquility, and our ambitions. Consequently, we have access to all the resources. However, the individuals we surround ourselves with are not the only ones determining who we become.

Because of what we do, we become acquainted with the individuals in our immediate environment. The things we accomplish are much more crucial. Because our work requires us to interact with other people, these people help establish the standard for what we consider to be acceptable, what we believe to be achievable, and what we are exposed to in our daily lives.

If we are dissatisfied with our surroundings, some effective strategies to effect change include taking up new pastimes, forming new routines, and reading new books—something that pushes us to our limits in the physical, mental, or spiritual realms. And by doing this, as well as finding something that we are passionate about and congruent with our core beliefs, we will meet the kinds of people with whom we want to surround ourselves.

Therefore, it is imperative to surround ourselves with people who assist in the realization of our visions, and one method to accomplish this is by engaging in enjoyable activities. Now that we have that out of the way, let's look at how successful and outstanding people achieve this.

How Successful People Use Successful People

Nobody matures into a witty, wise, or successful person by themselves. The surroundings that people put themselves in are of the utmost importance.

Although Elon Musk is a great thinker and has an incredible capacity for learning new things quickly, the success of his business is mostly because he surrounds himself with the most talented people possible in each of their particular fields.

There are several "mafias" in the field of technology. These mafias are collaborative networks of entrepreneurs who, based on a previously successful partnership, have begun new ventures together or have continued advising and investing in each other's business.

Reid Hoffman, who started LinkedIn, has made cultivating these relationships a primary focus of his professional life and encourages others to do the same. Because as he contends, in this day and age of knowledge, it is not about what we know but rather who we know that determines success. We have to figure out how to construct a network and then use that network to obtain the information we require. Getting information directly from those who have already accomplished what we wish to achieve is highly beneficial, as this information cannot just be obtained on Google.

Tim Ferris, a renowned author and entrepreneur who refers to himself as a "human guinea pig," uses a similar method. He chooses the individuals he hangs out with, following the aspect of his life that he feels needs the most improvement. Whether in the realm of the physical, the emotional, the psychological, or the financial, he locates the appropriate individuals. He spends a few months socializing with them before deciding that it is time to move on to something else.

What we can take away from successful people is the lesson that we need to be highly selective with how we use our time. Every minute we spend with one person is a minute we cannot spend with another person. The value of our time cannot be overstated. Therefore, it is preferable to spend it on those who can assist us in accomplishing our objectives.

On the other side, cultivating relationships takes time, so you must also be sure to commit the necessary amount of time.

How Do We Get Things Rolling?

Consider the people you spend the most time with, such as your friends and coworkers: do they encourage you, validate you, or bring you down?

To just exclude friends from one's life, as Gary Vaynerchuk recommends we ought to do, is not a course of action that I mainly support. On the other hand, we ought to be more thankful for them because they led us to where we are now. We should prioritize surrounding ourselves with individuals who share our passions and values and can assist us in achieving our objectives.

Ultimately, everything boils down to striking a balance since having your critics is necessary to test and validate your beliefs. However, it is crucial to strike a balance between the two.

This quip made by the boxer Frank Shamrock, who said that everyone requires the +, –, and =, is one of my favorites. He stated that for a fighter to grow into a great ones, they needed to have someone superior to them who they could learn from, someone who was inferior to them who they could teach, and someone equal to them who they could test themselves against.

Getting outside of my comfort zone or "bubble" has, in many ways, reshaped my perspective of the wider world. I've discovered that I genuinely enjoy trying out new things. I get a lot of enjoyment from interacting with people who come from very different backgrounds or hold quite different opinions, as well as attempting new activities and reading about new topics. They force me to reevaluate my preconceived notions and teach me something new; if I enjoy further information, I continue to pursue it. Every person I speak to teaches me something new and contributes to the enhancement of my life. This has led me to where I am now, but it will not serve as a final destination because I will always be interested in discovering what is out there.

It comes down to being clear about yourself and articulating those goals and values and what you stand for. And once that happens, opportunities and the right individuals will find their way to you.

CHAPTER 5

You Do You to Be Who You Are

'll start with the bad news: I need to find out the answer to the question that was asked earlier. I can listen to your concerns, accept you for who you are, nod in agreement, or give you a sympathetic pat on the back. However, I am unable to reveal your identity to you. You can only accomplish that. (Or perhaps astrologers can achieve that? I have no idea. As I said, not my department.)

The good news is that most individuals are already aware of who they are and what brings them joy, according to my uninformed and unscientific perspective. They might not know the steps necessary to become that person or achieve that life, but that is why I am here. And even if you don't know who you are and what you want off the top of your head, you could figure it out if you were allowed to do so, and there was no pressure from any outside source whatsoever. (Have I mentioned that I would be relying on you to complete that task before proceeding?)

However, you shouldn't worry about it because discovering who you are isn't quite as scary as it may sound. Playing "Who do you think you are?" is very similar to playing a video game, and anyone, even a seven-year-old with attention deficit hyperactivity disorder (ADHD), can do so.

In many video games, choosing a character is the first thing you do when you start playing. As an illustration, let's look at the timeless go-kart racing game *Mario Kart* from Nintendo. (You do not need any prior knowledge of *Mario Kart* to follow along with the rest of this article; however, kudos are in order if you have played the game and achieved the highest score on the "Bowser's Castle" level.)

In *Mario World*, you can play as Princess Peach, who rides quickly but loses control easily when struck, or as Bowser, a slow and methodical Koopa who doesn't get frightened when other players get up in your grill. (Koopas are anthropomorphic turtles with human characteristics. Again, not my department.) You can also be one of two unflappable Italian brothers who spend their weekdays operating a prosperous plumbing business and their weekends unwinding at the racetrack. Both Mario and Luigi are only along for the journey at this point.

You choose your player character depending on the character's abilities (in exchange, you accept the character's limitations). Which one suits your playing style and yields the most beneficial results?

The next thing to do in the game is select a "world" you want to play in. In *Mario Kart*, it would be a racetrack like Ghost Valley, Mushroom Gorge, or Moo Moo Meadows, among many others. There are a lot of different tracks. Each offers several positive and negative aspects, but determining which one you choose to play is how much fun it is for *you*.

In life, you also have the option to select between several different paths, such as being a family guy in the suburbs, a world traveler on the global stage, a philanthropist, an excellent athlete, or the champion of a hot dog–eating contest. Because analogies are not perfect and real life is more complicated than a video game, you can play more than one simultaneously. No matter what, only you can determine which one (or ones) provides you the most joy.

All set? Okay, now that we've gotten that out of the way, let's talk about what you can expect once you leave the two-dimensional boundaries of *Mario World*:

Do you plan your path, create your character, and focus on your best qualities when confronted with real-life situations that will affect your level of happiness? Or do you accept the position that the computer has assigned to you?

Do you sense that your decisions provide you with comfort, safety, and confidence? Or are you just trying to make it through the race in the middle of the pack without being knocked off the road by an animal with human characteristics?

These are the challenging questions, and sure, I did lull you into submission before sneaking them in here. However, there is no need for you to write down your responses because we are already aware of them. If you were playing to your strengths and felt comfortable, safe, and confident in your choices, then you would be out there kicking Koopa's ass and taking Koopa's names rather than reading this book and sucking nacho cheese dust off your fingers. If you were playing to your strengths, you would feel comfortable, safe, and confident in your choices.

No, if you're still listening to me at this point, I'm going to guess that the issue you're having isn't with who you are or what brings you joy; instead, the problem is that you get the impression that it's inappropriate to be that person and to want those things. No, if you're still listening to me at this point, I'm going to guess that the issue you're having isn't with who you are or what brings you joy; instead, the problem is that you get the impression that it's inappropriate to be that person and to want those things.

The question is, What gives you that impression? Because other people are constantly telling you that you are too loud, too quiet, too big, too small, too crazy, too weird, too selfish, too complicated, and too negative, that's probably why.

Using the Social Contract to Become a Better You

As soon as we emerge from the birth canal, we become subject to a predetermined code of conduct for humans, which we all (more or less) agree to adhere to live our lives in peace.

The so-called social contract is not a legal document and is not even a tangible one. However, the fact that its clauses have yet to be printed out and put in a fireproof safe-deposit box along with all our other critical documentation does not mean that we are unaware that they exist.

We are all required to share space in the world, whether on a highway, in a dorm room, or the pit at a Jamiroquai concert.

Unfortunately, sh*t happens sometimes that puts our ability for reason and self-control to the test. During such moments, the social contract is a buffer against our more primitive instincts. It prevents us from engaging in road rage, keeps us off the dean's "shit list," and prevents us from using a lighter to set fire to the hair of the girl who pushed her way in front of us at the venue even though we had been there for hours before she and her oblivious friend showed up. It also steers us away from the brink of road rage.

And I wholeheartedly concur that there are specific guidelines that each of us ought to follow, such as "Do not pull out your cell phone in the middle of a Broadway musical," "Do not answer the door naked when folks come a-caroling," and "Do not post unflattering photos of your friends on social media."

However, there are other provisions, and quite a few, to which we must not adhere "simply because." Some of them have the potential to injure us more than they can assist others; some of them are out of date, out of style, or out of touch; and some of them threaten to upset the very balance that the social compact was put in place to protect.

I picked fifteen of the ones I disliked the most to concentrate on, such as "Don't be selfish" and "You will regret that," and I changed them to apply to a much broader section of the population. This includes, but is not limited to, people who are weird, pessimistic, loners, hot messes, and most certainly will not regret that, but I appreciate your concern.

The Social Contract and All That Comes Along with It

- *Don't be so self-centered!* It is not only acceptable but also beneficial to be worried about your self-interest, which you may do while also looking out for the interests of others. Being selfish and having a selfless nature are not necessarily incompatible states.
- *Give it your all.* Even if you have admirable traits, such as ambition and ethics, achieving anything is difficult while

both hands are engaged in scratching the hives that stress has caused.

- *Don't put yourself through that!* Take a stand not only for yourself but also for others. Being "difficult" is not the same as having the courage of your convictions. It is a commendable act, and in addition, it will get you a better table.
- *Be sure to contribute to the team.* If going your way gets your bacon frying, go for it. Who the hell gives a fuck how you do it as long as the task is completed?
- *Don't quit your day job.* Foster a positive outlook on taking risks, and don't let the naysayers and critics deter you from doing so when the moment is right. Also, fear is another name for putting a large blue tarp over your head and stifling your dreams.
- *You are going to have a change of heart.* Maybe, but if you do, no issue. Do not let other people's viewpoints regarding the decisions you have made in your life, particularly the "unconventional" ones, prevent you from being authentic to who you are.
- *That kind of mentality is not going to get you very far.* The perfect mentality for you is the one that gives you energy, gives you a sense of security, and helps you get a good night's sleep tonight so you can wake up and enjoy your vacation tomorrow.
- *You will come to regret doing that.* If at first someone's attempts to change your thinking are unsuccessful, they will try and try again by filling your head with stories of potential misfortune. Ignore what they have to say.
- *If you don't go to college, it will be tricky for you to find decent employment.* Your idea of success is all that matters. Nobody needs a certificate, either in the natural or figurative sense, to tell them what feels good.
- *That will haunt you for the rest of your life.* Clap your hands if you are aware that you are a strange person. And even if that's not the case, a polite round of applause for the rest of us wouldn't go amiss.

- *You should always prioritize spending time with your family.* Please don't hesitate to give the same amount of value to each of the lovely individuals in your life. There, wasn't that too much trouble?
- *You need to tone it down.* It is just as vital to take care of your mental health as your physical health, and if doing so requires you to be transparent about how you do so, by all means, do so.
- *You shouldn't put something in your mouth.* Instead of criticizing your body for what it isn't, try learning to appreciate it for what it is. And save me some pizza.
- *You need to leave your pride outside of the door.* Who else will have trust in you if you don't have it in yourself? Own it, talk with it, walk with it, and don't forget to celebrate yourself daily. Own it, talk with it, and walk with it. You are deserving of it.
- *Put your family first.* It's easy to make excuses to avoid spending time with family. Work, school, and other obligations can often take priority over the ones we love. But what if we took a step back and prioritized our families? Putting your family first strengthens relationships and brings peace of mind when the rest of life is hectic.

  Making your family a priority isn't limited to those living under one roof; it also applies to extended families. Taking time out for family lunches or game nights encourages connection and communication between relatives who may live far apart. It also creates lasting memories that will be cherished forever! This doesn't have to be expensive either; many activities are free or require a minimal investment of resources.

  Take some time today to prioritize your loved ones and watch how it positively impacts all areas of your life!

PART 2

WHO DO YOU SEE IN THE MIRROR?

CHAPTER 6

Understanding the Mirror and How to Use It to Shape Who You Want to Be

Mirrors have the power to make us feel a wide range of emotions, and they also have the potential to be highly effective instruments for shifting our point of view and illuminating aspects of ourselves that are typically obscured when we look out into the world.

It is fundamental and inbuilt in us to have the need to be seen and reflected upon. When we are young, we gain an understanding of who we are by observing ourselves reflected in the people around us. Researchers in psychology have discovered that direct interpersonal interaction is necessary to grow our social and emotional skills. We miss out on opportunities for social contemplation as we spend more time alone and occupy ourselves with our electronic devices. We can have an immediate face-to-face encounter with ourselves anytime if we have access to a mirror.

One of the practices I've developed is using a mirror in meditation to gain a more compassionate knowledge of oneself and increase one's capacity for resilience in facing life's challenges.

Discovering how to tune into your image will not transform you into a narcissist of towering proportions. On the contrary, this experience will teach you how to be more present with yourself, how to manage the intensity of your emotions better, and how to access fresh wells of inner strength. Kinder self-awareness is the key to breaking free from the inner critic and the external world that stokes our fears and anxieties that we are never safe, never good enough, and never have enough. These two sources fuel our fears and concerns that we will never be safe, good enough, and never have enough.

Learning about Who You Are by Looking at Who You Are

When I was a little boy, I liked to stare at my reflection on the side of the bright chrome toaster sitting on the table. I was mesmerized by the different expressions that appeared on my face, and I would often exaggerate them to mimic the adults' behaviors in the room. Observing my reflection provided me with a source of fun and interest, in addition to assisting me in comprehending and expressing my feelings. I could observe not just how I felt but also how I appeared when experiencing those feelings. This seemed to calm me down and was also reassuring in some way.

As I became older, I learned, as most of us do, to use the mirror to monitor my look and analyze it based on cultural standards of beauty, finding infinite defects and blemishes along the way. This is something that most of us do. When I needed a moment to catch my breath, I occasionally glanced into my eyes and wondered, *Who was I?* What were the true depths of my emotions?

The other day, I happened to catch a glimpse of my face in the mirror, and I was astonished to see how miserable and troubled I appeared. I had hardly recognized that I felt that way, assuming I was "great." I realized that I had been building a picture of myself that I believed would appeal to other people, and as a result, I had lost touch with how I felt inside. This was a startling realization for me.

Discovering how to tune into your image will not transform you into a narcissist of towering proportions. On the contrary, this experience will teach you how to be more present with yourself, how to manage the intensity of your emotions better, and how to access fresh wells of inner strength.

I started making it a habit to acknowledge my presence and get in touch with how I was feeling by taking a few moments each day to look at my reflection in the mirror. This wasn't so that I could critique my appearance or try to picture how I appeared to others; instead, it was so that I could simply acknowledge myself. As I continued to do this over time, I discovered a method to look past the flaws in my appearance and see deeper into my own eyes with compassion. This was a massive step for me. It turned into a time for reflection, a method for merely existing at the moment, with no agenda other than to be in the room with me.

Simply scheduling time each day to give myself my complete and undivided attention has become a priceless luxury for me amid my hectic existence. I was looking forward to having some time to myself when I could just rest and unwind in my own company.

But doing so was not an act of adoring oneself in any way.

I didn't just sit there and blow kisses to myself the whole time. Instead, it was a check-in to see how I felt about myself, my appearance, my emotions, and the many different dramas in my life. My features divulged a great deal, some concealed from plain view. I trained myself to focus on myself regardless of how I was feeling or how many other things were going on in my life that were competing for my attention. I saw a significant shift after doing this mirror meditation for at least ten minutes per day for more than a year, and people around me noticed the same thing.

I used to be quite self-conscious about my appearance, but as time went on, I learned to approach myself in a way that was more natural, accepting, and kind to myself. As a result, I grew less self-conscious about my appearance. In addition to that, I came to the mirror so that I might use it to help me deal with the difficulties and diversions of daily life.

I stopped looking outside of myself for people, places, or things that would distract me from negative emotions or self-criticism. Instead, I used the mirror to face myself and ground myself by simply looking into my eyes with compassion. This helped me stop searching for people, places, and things that would distract me from negative emotions or self-criticism. I discovered that looking in the mirror was an excellent method to work through my feelings. When I was fighting with unpleasant thoughts and no one could provide a caring ear—or when I just didn't want to offend anyone or say something I'd regret saying afterward—the mirror became a powerful reflector of my anguish and suffering during those times.

The reflection in the mirror provided a vantage point that I could not see from within my mind. I had a perception of myself that was frequently in a state far too raw and exposed for me to share with others. Instead of relying on affirmations from other people or validation from whatever I was currently defined as "success," I simply acknowledged myself unapologetically with love and compassion. When I looked in the mirror, I was often flooded with compassion and appreciation for how much I do and how hard I try. I was already deserving of love and compassion simply by existing. Therefore, I didn't need to do anything to earn it.

My reasons for connecting with other people became crystal clear: it was less about getting others to see me, affirm me, and think I was fantastic and more about finding who they genuinely are, as well as what they are sending beyond their words.

My internal critic would occasionally speak up and ask, "Isn't this a little bit narcissistic?" "Aren't you being a bit self-centered here?" "Instead of staring at yourself in the mirror, shouldn't you concentrate on assisting those less fortunate?" When I took the time to pause and evaluate these criticisms and ask myself how mirror gazing affected my relationships and general approach to life, I found that it had caused a significant shift in my perspective. The irony, however, was that when I took the time to look at myself in the mirror, I was more interested in developing meaningful connections with others rather than less.

Why? My reasons for connecting with other people became crystal clear: it was less about getting others to see me, affirm me, and think I was fantastic and more about finding who they genuinely are, as well as what they are sending beyond their words. It is a well-known proverb that there are two sides to a conversation: the side that is talking and the side that is waiting to talk. It is possible that in our haste to see, be acknowledged, and be understood by one another, we will utterly miss one another. Focusing our attention inward allows us to be compassionate toward other people while also tending to our emotional well-being.

How to Practice the Mirror Meditation

Because I found the mirror to be such a helpful instrument, I decided to recommend it to other people. I have been instructing others in mirror meditation for the past seven years. Students meditate on their reflections by using mirror gazing and the concepts of mindfulness meditation in conjunction with each other.

The vast majority of people, at first glance, appear to be exceedingly awkward and self-conscious. Their eyes are harsh and judgmental as they glance at themselves in the mirror, causing their faces to stiffen as they tweak this and that. Then when they discuss what they are going through, I help them go beyond their outward appearance, set aside the stories they tell themselves regularly, and take a more in-depth look at who they are. I want people to look at themselves not as the person they are criticizing but as the person suffering rather than the object of their criticism. Frequently, they can redirect their attention away from recognizing their flaws and toward seeing themselves in the mirror as the one who is suffering and the one who is responsible for the pain. There is an audible snap. In most cases, by the time the session is through, their faces have softened, and over time, they appear more peaceful and self-accepting, nicer to themselves, and more trusting of their own experience.

These shifts have, on occasion, been nothing short of miraculous. People can cut through their self-delusions and develop kinder and more accurate self-awareness when they take the time to give themselves their full attention. Many people have reported deep insights into how they see themselves and how it influences their lives by simply taking the time to provide their full attention. Some people have discovered that it is an effective instrument for supporting their development programs, such as psychotherapy, life coaching, addiction treatment, and support groups for people going through life transitions.

I invited my students practicing mirror gazing to describe, in their own words, any changes they experienced as a result of conducting the meditation as we went along with the program. After analyzing the content of these written comments, three recurring topics emerged as clear favorites. And the mirror revealed exactly how much their critiques were affecting them because they could see it on their face, which showed just how much the criticisms were affecting them.

The first thing that happened was that they became conscious of the extent to which they were self-critical, whether it pertained to their physical appearance or some other facet of themselves that they routinely felt lacking. The mirror helped to illuminate the situation. And the mirror revealed how much their criticisms were affecting them because they could see it on their face, which was a revelation in and of itself! After that, they were given the opportunity and practice to show themselves greater acceptance and compassion.

You will become more conscious of how you are feeling moment to moment since the mirror reflects your facial emotions, and it can be startling for anybody at first. The mirror can also reflect your facial expressions. Some people can become more conscious of the feelings they normally try to suppress, such as fear, wrath, or disgust, which they have not been aware of in the past. You will discover that as a result of practicing meditation, you can feel and accept a wider variety of emotions than before.

How and Why Mirror Meditation Is Effective

Why is looking in the mirror such a powerful and successful technique? As I dove deeper into the study of neuroscience and psychology, the pieces of the puzzle started to fall into place. According to research, face-to-face interaction is necessary for developing a sense of self, the ability to manage emotions, and the capacity to empathize with others. The reflections of others help us understand who we are as individuals. And by looking at their faces, we can understand how they feel and how we, in turn, feel. We get into the habit of adjusting our expressions on a moment-to-moment basis according to how they respond to us. This is the groundwork that must be laid before we can learn to control our feelings and negotiate difficult social circumstances.

We miss out on the face-to-face reflection that helps us stay emotionally connected to ourselves as we spend more time alone and on our devices. As a result, we become more emotionally disconnected from ourselves. The mirror can potentially be a beneficial instrument in preserving that connection. The quality of the relationship that we have with ourselves can be seen reflected in the mirror. My line of work has shown me that individuals can be callous to themselves without even being aware of it, which is a phenomenon that I find astounding. Our self-criticism is reflected in the mirror with pinpoint precision. Then we are allowed to choose to be nice to ourselves and have the chance to practice doing so.

How to Perform the Mirror Meditation

Daily mirror gazing should consist of ten minutes of complete silence. Here are some simple guidelines:

- *Create the environment and the intention.* You should select a well-lit location, free of distractions, and where you can arrange a mirror so that it is freestanding. This will allow you to look into your eyes without strain or bending forward. Place both feet firmly on the ground and sit cross-legged on a meditation cushion or chair. Put ten minutes on the timer that you just set. You should not set goals aside from simply spending the specified time with yourself.
- *Bring your attention to how you breathe.* Start by closing both of your eyes. Focus on your breathing for a moment. Are you short of breath or have a high breathing rate? Take a few calm, deep breaths into your stomach. Then

maintain a regular and natural breathing pattern, focusing on how your breath makes your belly, rib cage, and collarbones move as you inhale and then noticing how your breath makes your collarbones, rib cage, and belly softly contract as you exhale. Become aware of any tense regions of your body, paying particular attention to your face and shoulders, and then picture sending your breath to relax those areas and allow the tension to dissolve.

- *Direct your sight inward, into your own eyes.* When you initially look at yourself, pay attention to whether or not your breathing changes. Bring your breathing back up to a full, steady level. Take note of the nature of your stare, noticing if it is harsh or gentle. Make an effort to look less intense. If you become more rigid due to concentrating on a particular aspect of your appearance or a defect, try deep breathing exercises until you sense that your body is again beginning to relax.

- *Pay attention to your critics.* Notice your eyes as you look at yourself in this exacting, maybe even harsh or cold way. Try to see if you can switch your attention from the person (or image in the mirror) that you are scrutinizing to seeing the person who is underneath receiving that scrutiny; that is who you are. If your initial reaction to looking at yourself is critical, notice your eyes as you look at yourself in this exacting, maybe even harsh or cold way. When you receive criticism about a specific aspect of yourself, how does it make you feel?

- *Take note of where your attention wanders and the feelings that accompany it.* Look at your reflection while keeping an open mind to whatever comes up. Take note of any feelings or emotions that surface; without attaching any meaning, simply let them exist in the present moment. Simply allow your thoughts and feelings to float as you focus on your breathing, try to relax your body, and look in the mirror without any other intention than to be present with yourself. Pay attention to whether your focus gets narrow and exact, and if it does, see if you can broaden it so that you can see your entire body, your entire self, and any expressions of emotion on your face. Observe how your attention is growing and contracting, as well as the thoughts and images that are entering your head now. Simply be aware of where your attention wanders and any feelings that may be connected to it without passing judgment. While engaging in the activity, you should maintain a compassionate attitude toward yourself. Within ten minutes, your perspective on yourself can shift profoundly, which might surprise you.

PART 3

UNDERSTANDING THE NOW TO PLAN FOR TOMORROW

CHAPTER 7

The Power of the Moment

Starting off with these three quotes, you will learn to understand the importance of how the moment you are living now should be held with importance.

> Both the life we live in our thoughts and the life we experience in the current moment are separate lives that we lead.

> Our existence in ideas begins to fade as our perception of the present moment takes over.

> Learning to balance ideas with the present moment is the path to freedom.

When we recall an experience, we tend to remember flagship moments: the highs, the falls, and the transformations. A defining moment is a typical short, memorable, and meaningful experience. Elevation, insight, pride, and connections are all elements or components from which defining moments can be created.

If you're struggling to transition, create a defining moment that draws a dividing line between the present you, which would become the *old you*, and the intending you, the *new you*, you would become.

Transitions should be marked, milestones commemorated, and full of falls; it is a rocky path mostly.

In the Now

The power in moments exposes you to experiences such as how and why specific fleeting encounters may uplift, shock, and transform you and enable you to learn to create such amazing moments in your personal and professional lives.

According to research, when we recall an experience, we tend to overlook the majority of the details and concentrate instead on a select few key moments.

The term *duration neglect* refers to the tendency for individuals to overlook or forget the length of an experience while evaluating it. Instead, we evaluate the experience based on two crucial points:

- the peak, either high or low
- the conclusion

This is termed the "peak-end rule" by psychologists.

Undeniably, we do not average our minute-by-minute sensations when we evaluate our experiences. Instead, we frequently recall high points, low points, and changes in direction, transition, or transformation. A typical example is forgetting outstanding customer service, which often stands out.

Some moments have a far greater significance than others. That is why you should not forget.

> A defining moment is both
> memorable and significant.

Using this understanding, four factors can combine to produce memorable moments:

Elevation

Witnessing real or imagined virtuous deeds of exceptional moral virtue may elevate one's mood. It is a distinct sensation of warmth and expansion, accompanied by admiration and love for the person whose unusual behavior is being seen. Elevation inspires individuals who experience it to connect with, join, and help others. One feels uplifted and enthusiastic about mankind when they are elevated.

Insight

Insight is the foundation of innovation since
it is the creative force that generates fresh ideas.

According to studies, insight doesn't just appear out of nowhere; it's the product of the unconscious mind putting disparate pieces of knowledge from previous experiences together in innovative ways. Naturally, analogies between insight and creativity arise from this notion of insight. In contrast, creativity requires several cognitive processes across the brain and cannot be lateralized. During creative issue-solving, insight may unquestionably lead to original solutions. In an insightful moment, we often slip over the truth and lean for understanding.

Pride

A prideful moment is filled with a legitimate sense of self-worth or satisfaction because of one's own or another's accomplishment.

When you feel proud, you are happy about something positive that you have or have done or that someone close to you has accomplished. With a prideful moment comes the acknowledgment of others, and you can set new milestones while also building self-confidence.

Connection

We get bonded through our shared experiences. When a group works together to achieve a worthwhile objective, they get stronger; they experience a "synchronized moment." Responsiveness strengthens our bonds in personal interactions. People may come together quite fast through a responsive relationship.

Defining moments possess at least one of the four elements listed above. However, it could be a mix of all four components.

Facing Reality

You've stumbled over the truth when you experience an unexpected insight that you didn't see coming but that you know in your gut is accurate. It's a turning point that has the power to alter your perspective on the world in an instant.

It is often accompanied by an experience of the "aha" moment.

In having to face reality, this three-part formula often helps us navigate through the process:

- Clear understanding
- Compressed in time
- Uncovered by the individual itself

The problem must first be understood before the solution can be appreciated. Chip and Dan refer to the truth about an issue or injury when they write about "stepping over the truth." That is what prompts an epiphanic epiphany.

Through Insights

According to research, brooding or thinking about our ideas and emotions can be more helpful for achieving deep insight. It is more productive to examine our actions.

More frequently than insight leads to action, action leads to insight.

One of the researchers who popularized the "peak-end principle," Barbara Fredrickson, asserted that people prioritize peaks in memory because they act as a mental price tag. In essence, they warn us this is what it may cost you to go through that ordeal once more.

Students' natural responses may be defensiveness or skepticism when they receive their book that is filled with errors and suggestions. "The teacher has never liked me." But the insightful critique note conveys a different point of view. It implies that you can achieve great things if you put in the necessary effort. There is no bias in the essay that has been marked up. It takes effort to stretch.

"I have high expectations for you, and I know you can reach them," a mentor might say. Therefore, give this new task a go; if you fail, I'll assist you in bouncing back.

When a mentor pushes you, you stretch and get a revelation about yourself.

Realizations and changes come from epiphanies. They don't have to be coincidental. We can cause someone to "trip over the truth," which refers to triggering an emotional realization to provide them with moments of insight.

We must extend ourselves by putting ourselves in novel situations that put us in danger of failing to generate moments of self-insight.

Mentors can encourage us to push ourselves further than we previously believed possible, and in the process, they can inspire pivotal moments.

The recipe for mentoring that promotes self-awareness is high standards plus confidence plus direction plus support.

We must fight against our innate desire to keep the people we care about safe to hold our mentees accountable for stretching. to shield them.

Stretching has the promise of learning rather than accomplishment.

Elevating moments help us rise above the mundane. Aha moments lead to new understandings about the world and ourselves. Moments of pride catch us at our best—displaying courage, receiving praise, and overcoming obstacles.

Being Intentional

Being purposeful is giving something vital to you your dedication, attention, and concentration. You must be clear and upfront about what you want to accomplish and then take action to make it happen if you want to be purposeful every day.

This short tutorial explains what it is to be purposeful and offers six tips for being deliberate in your behavior, thoughts, and deeds.

You can improve your capacity to be purposeful every day, and it will impact your life. Being deliberate about what is essential to you and acting on those things will be two guiding traits to take your life ahead and achieve development every day.

By being deliberate, you may become more present and accomplish more and better goals in your company and personal life. Being deliberate gives your day a distinct direction, order, and a good attitude.

What does the word *intention* mean? It implies that you are purposeful about acting on the ideas and emotions that are most significant to you and that you have a clear goal. When you choose to build a life with a clear purpose that is important and exciting to you, you choose to have an intentional focus.

By acting on the things that are significant to you, you may learn to be more purposeful. Living with intention is making deliberate decisions to live your desired life rather than letting other people control your thoughts, feelings, and behavior.

If you're an intentional person, everything you do has a specific goal. When you are deliberate, you don't allow fear to hold you back; instead, you concentrate your time and efforts on your assets and the positive aspects of your life.

Intentional people are action-oriented, unwavering in their resolve, and committed to achieving their goals. It's crucial to be self-aware, to say no more often than you say yes, and to cultivate thankfulness if you want to become more purposeful.

With intention, you may cultivate gratitude for essential things in your life and increase your appreciation for them. When you build stronger boundaries around your time and the critical aspects of your life, you are being deliberate.

When you are deliberate, you achieve a lot. But the question remains, How do you become intentional and purposeful daily?

Strategies to Becoming Deliberate Each Day

Take your time and plan your day.

You are far more likely to get the desired outcome when you intentionally use your time, energy, and concentration daily. By being deliberate with your time, you can create daily routines that complement your goals and guarantee that your day has a defined framework.

You can better direct your time and attention when you have more outstanding direction and purpose. Your larger mission and the use of your time are in alignment, which boosts creativity and productivity.

With a planned focus for the day, you can feel free and save time on trivial pursuits. You may take on too much without meaning to and get easily sidetracked.

Choose the three crucial tasks that will help you accomplish your desired result to help you plan your day more carefully. You'll indeed feel pleased with what you've accomplished, which will increase your confidence and self-esteem.

A deliberate commitment to what you want guarantees that your activities align with your objectives and that you concentrate your time on your top priorities.

Be specific about the desired outcome.

Clarifying the quantifiable outcomes you hope to attain in the future can help you become more purposeful. You will be more intentional when you are confident of the desired results and realize how crucial it is to get there.

Your motivation and attention are focused on taking action when your vision and measurable goals are in line. Get crystal clear about the desired result through practical goal setting to be more intentional. To comprehend the significance of your dreams, visualize yourself having attained them.

You act deliberately when you have an emotional stake in your larger purpose and ambitions. Your confidence will grow as you visualize your life after reaching your objectives, inspiring you daily.

Make good use of your time.

Being deliberate is all about using your time wisely to advance your most significant objectives. When you are purposeful with your time, your day has a defined framework, and you develop healthy daily routines and habits.

Intentional individuals are aware of the value of their time and strive to accomplish their objectives as quickly, simply, and efficiently as possible. Understanding which goals, connections, and teamwork will help you get the desired outcomes can help you be more purposeful with your time management.

Structure your schedule around your energy levels, limit your time, and schedule time for self-care. Your time will be better managed, and you'll feel more proud of your daily accomplishments if you begin and conclude each day with appreciation.

Pay attention and be thought of.

Your ability to focus on the people and things that matter most is increased by intention. By focusing your thoughts and activities on achieving your larger goal, intentionality helps you comprehend its significance and purpose.

An intentional focus helps you become more precise about what you want and removes the uncertainty about where to put your time and attention. By being deliberate with your attention, you can set priorities that are productive and create a schedule for your day that is focused on your more critical purpose.

Direct your attention to what is most important to you when you are confident in your vision and are aware of the necessary subsequent actions.

Concentrate on your objectives.

You may integrate your purpose and vision with an action plan to accomplish your goals by setting intentional goals. You gain more outstanding direction and concentration by identifying the outcome you want to attain when you are purposeful with your objectives.

By setting objectives, you can guarantee that each day begins with concentration and purpose and that you have a plan and a road to follow. Your dreams become more motivating and clear when you have goals to work toward.

You know why you want to attain your objectives and when you want to reach them when they are well-defined. You can plan your schedule with certainty thanks to this precision. Additionally, it enables you to focus your time and efforts on your top objectives.

Be aware of your most crucial relationships.

Your most significant connections get more worth and significance due to intentionality. When you cherish your most important connections, you feel more appreciation, affluence, and self-awareness.

It aids in your comprehension of each relationship's significance and goal. You feel better and more pleased when you take the time to understand why a connection is crucial.

A person becomes more valuable when you show thanks to them. Being clear on the best outcome you want from a relationship is ensured by knowing what you want from it.

Keeping in touch with the people who matter also demonstrates how much you appreciate the people around you.

CHAPTER 8

Planning for the Future while Living the Now

Maintaining a balance between living in the here and now and preparing for the future has been challenging. How can one simultaneously prepare for the future and live in the present?

We are continually inundated with messages telling us how vital each of these items is, and they are as follows:

You must make plans for the future since doing so will bring you success, satisfaction, and contentment in the long run. With a well-thought-out strategy, you'll likely make progress in the correct direction or be able to build the kind of life you see for yourself.

You have to make an effort to focus on the here and now to experience contentment, gratitude, and joy in your life. If you're constantly dwelling on the bad things or worrying about what may happen in the future, you'll lose out on the good things in your life right now.

It might be easier if you were just required to concentrate on one of these two aspects of the situation. When you try to do both at the same time, though, things can quickly become stressful and confusing for you. How can one live in the present while also planning for the future?

Some best practices you should follow can help you be present and enjoy your current life while also dreaming about and working toward a bigger and brighter future. Although different approaches will work for other people, there are some best practices that you should follow.

Self-Awareness

Self-awareness is essential to making any change in your life, and it can be of tremendous assistance when attempting to strike a balance between the past and the future.

There is a good chance that one of two things comes more readily to you: either living in the moment or making plans for the future. If you want to live a more balanced life, knowing which way you lean can be helpful. Are you more focused on the present or more interested in the future? Here is a quick reference guide to assist you in making your choice:

You may be more focused on the present and now if...

- It is difficult to conceive of the future as dissimilar to the present.
- When your objectives or plans become a reality, you tend to give up on achieving them.
- They are more spontaneous.
- You have regular FOMO (fear of missing out).
- You consider the possibility that the future will not go as planned, so refrain from making too many preparations.
- You'll drive yourself crazy dealing with folks who seem to value their careers more than the connections they've made.

You may have a better outlook on the future if...

- You should have no problem speculating about and talking about what the future might be like.
- Regularly establishing and achieving your goals should be a priority.
- You like to prepare ahead of time.

- You believe that the hard effort you put in today will pay you in the form of fun tomorrow.
- You have faith that (most of) your plans for the future will come to fruition.
- You are angered by the behavior of those who appear to have no work ethic.

Present You versus Future You

When I was chatting with a friend about this topic, they told me they were having an ongoing conversation with their therapist. They talked about a "future self" and a "present self," almost as if they were two distinct individuals, and they talked about how important it was to give both of those "selves" a voice. They also spoke about how essential it was to give both of those "selves" a voice.

My friend's "future self" directed most of their actions for most of the period. This meant that some wonderful things would happen, such as my friend is an exceptional manager, strategist, and planner. But it also caused considerable exhaustion, unhappiness, and a feeling of "not experiencing life," which resulted from the toll it took in significant ways.

The important thing is not to allow the "you" that is naturally in charge too much authority and to ensure that the other version still has a voice in the conversation.

My friend had to learn the hard way that happiness and sanity are not something to be sacrificed to achieve one's ambitions. They were required to communicate with their "current selves."

Others might need to be taught that ignoring their "future selves" in favor of instant gratification is likely to result in a lack of long-term fulfillment and that this is a lesson they need to learn. It is critical to consider what the future you have to say.

When you become conscious of the part of yourself that is typically in command, you will be better able to recognize when you are silencing a part of yourself that could assist you.

SMART Objectives

When attempting to plan for the future while still living in the present, awareness is vital, but it does not mean much unless followed by action.

Setting SMART objectives is one of the most beneficial things you can do for yourself. Setting goals is very much an activity that involves planning for the future; however, making sure that your goals are SMART enables you to strike a balance between the life you are living now and the one you are planning for the future.

A SMART goal is a goal that is designed to maximize your chances of success.

SMART goals are as follows:

- *Specific.* Clearly defines the goal and your desired outcomes
- *Measurable.* Allows you to track your progress and know when you've succeeded
- *Achievable.* Realistic, something you can do.
- *Relevant.* Falls in line with your overall vision for your life
- *Time-based.* Includes a deadline to help you stay on track.

Why Does Adhering to the SMART Framework Make It Possible for You to Continue Living in the Future while Also Making Plans for the Future?

Because setting SMART objectives is meant to be manageable and not to leave you feeling disheartened or overwhelmed. When you have a distinct purpose that you are optimistic you will be able to achieve and that is relevant to your life, you will have reasonable expectations, which will help you feel confident in your plans. You are convinced that you have established reasonable goals for yourself. As a result, you do not need to expend any of your current energy attempting to figure out how to achieve goals that are either too imprecise or too ambitious.

Simply said, making an effort to formulate your objectives as SMART goals frees up more of your time and energy in the here and now. It will bring you where you want to go, but it will also allow you to live your life while you are traveling there.

Develop plans that can be carried out.

Along these same lines, having plans that have been consciously made and are actionable may help you blend your present self with your future self.

One further approach to look at this would be to consider it in terms of choosing behaviors that will benefit you in the here and now and in the future. Which step can you take right now that, in addition to keeping you present in the here and now, will also fulfill your desire to "create happiness" in the years to come?

Because it is not always easy to detect these acts immediately away, drawing backward is something that we recommend doing.

Which is more important, where you are right now or where you want to be in the future? It is the latter. If you have a clear idea of where you want to end up, it doesn't matter where you are; you can still get there. This is the concept behind drawing backward; you start at the end and work your way back until you've successfully connected all the dots leading up to your current state.

Drawing backward should eventually bring you to a step you can take right now, and when you do take that step, you should feel confident that it has been meticulously crafted to lead you in the direction you desire.

You can enjoy your life in the here and now while still making progress toward achieving your goals for the future because you have such a solid strategy in place. Because you will know that you have already established a plan to reach your destination, you won't have to spend as much time worrying about the future. At the same time, you won't merely be living for the moment; instead, you'll be proactively heading in the proper path. This is the equilibrium that each of us is striving to achieve.

Track your learning.

Using Veron Howard's quote, "Always walk through life as if you have something new to learn, and you will," you will understand why it is essential to track your life and learning.

Every day, we are given opportunities to learn from life. The question is whether or not we truly take anything away from those experiences.

Daily, we are given a chance to expand our knowledge in various domains, including interpersonal dynamics, personal development, and the operation of the global system. There are a few of these teachings that are so profound that they completely take us by surprise. Some are pretty intricate, so we can hardly recognize them. However, each can teach us something useful in the future.

When you keep an eye out for opportunities to improve your knowledge, you strike a balance between the here and now and the potential benefits of the future. Recognizing those lessons enables you to be more present in the here and now and more aware of what transpired, how you felt, how it impacted others, and what you gained from experience. After that, you can use that knowledge in the future. You are managing your life here and now while preparing for the future.

Every day should be viewed as an opportunity to learn something new. You may write down one lesson you learn daily, regardless of how big or minor it is. Getting into this routine will make it easier for you to detect them, and it will also make it easier for you to find patterns that could make the teachings even more profound and essential.

Keep your ideas under control.

Your thoughts create the world you experience. Every idea you have affects you, altering your disposition, motivating you to take action, or causing you to behave differently toward another person. This may either help us or hurt us in the long run. Our thoughts have the power to either motivate us toward doing good and positive change or to lead us down roads that are unproductive or even dangerous.

Your thoughts can be concentrated on preparing for the future or enjoying life in the here and now for this essay. What you believe dictates where you put your energy and how it manifests itself. Where you place your energy is directly proportional to what you think.

There is no denying the potency of one's thoughts, but there is something that is even more potent, and that is you. Your ideas are under your control at all times.

There are indeed moments when thoughts jump into our heads without us asking them to, and it is also true that this might happen. However, even if it does, you still can control that thinking. What exactly are you going to do with it? What kind of reaction do you have to it? Should you welcome that notion into your life, or is it something you should ignore? By making these choices, you allow yourself to construct your ideas to serve you and assist you in striking a balance between living in the here and now and planning for the future.

When you learn to command your thoughts, you give flight to your inner dragon and can put that ferocious creativity to work for you to bring about change in your life. You can detect when the ideas of your present-day self are doing your plans for the future a disservice and when your thoughts about the future are preventing you from experiencing your life to the fullest. You can mold your thoughts so that they are more well-balanced. Your ideas have the power to assist you in "creating happiness."

The ability to live in the now while preparing for the future must be honed through practice. You must become conscious of your inherent tendencies and work to combat them to succeed. You must learn to think in a way that will direct you to activities beneficial to your current and future selves. In addition, you will need to acquire the skill of drawing backward the gap between the life you see living in the future and the life you are living in the here and now.

Regarding focus, your history and your future are not alternatives that must be chosen between. Both of them belong to you. Claim them both, live them both, and be happy while you're at it while you're creating happiness for others.

CHAPTER 9

Balancing Futuristic and Current Goals

How Do You Balance Present-Day Activities with Long-Term Planning?

First, it should be clarified that being in the present does not imply separation from the past or the future. For instance, we may remain in the current moment while consciously recalling earlier occasions (as opposed to being caught up, distracted, and overwhelmed by the past).

Similarly, while intentionally making plans for the future, we may remain in the now (as opposed to being caught up, distracted, and overwhelmed by thoughts of the future).

Being present also means being aware of our needs, wants, and plans. Making plans may be done in the present rather than allowing our minds to wander. We are capable of being in the moment while thinking and recalling the past. Being present serves as a reminder to focus on the here and now, no matter what we do.

Living in the moment and making plans for the future simultaneously is a classic balancing act. How can you be present at the moment and plan simultaneously?

Constant signals tell us how important each of these things is separate:

You must make plans for the future if you want to attain your goals and find contentment. You won't likely proceed in the proper direction or build the life you want to live if you don't have a determined strategy.

> Fitting in is a short-term strategy that gets you nowhere. Standing out is a long-term strategy that takes guts and produces results. (Seth Godin)

Living in the moment is essential to find pleasure, appreciation, and calm. You'll miss your life occurring in front of you if you're perpetually down about the past or worried about the future.

It may not be so difficult if you only had to focus on one of these subjects. However, attempting to perform both at once may quickly become perplexing and stressful. How can you live in the now while making plans for the future?

There are some best practices to follow that will help you be present in the moment and appreciate your current life while simultaneously dreaming about and working toward a bigger, better future. While various strategies will work for different people, setting short- and long-term objectives is crucial. They are essential for professional success and can also be utilized to achieve equilibrium in personal affairs.

When you consider it, it makes logical sense. Since life may lead you in many different directions without clear and concrete objectives, it will be difficult for you to arrive where you want to be. You understand that failing to plan is planning to fail. Without both short-term and long-term goals, you are like a ship at sea without a course.

> Goals are a means to an end, not the ultimate purpose of our lives. They are simply a tool to concentrate our focus and move us in a direction. The only reason we pursue goals is to cause ourselves to expand and grow. (Tony Robbins)

But it's critical to understand that when setting realistic plans, there are two types of goals at work:

Long-term goals come first; they are your broad, overarching aims. "Owning a business," "becoming a neurosurgeon," or "purchasing your own home" can be included on a list of long-term objectives. How long-term are your objectives? Long-term objectives are substantial and take a long time to complete, which could range from three to five years or more.

> Having a long-term goal catalyzes motivation at every waking moment. (Peter J. Daniels)

Short-term goals, or "steps," are the second category of goals. What distinguishes short-term goals from long-term goals? Your short-term objectives are smaller subsets of your long-term goals and include the concrete activities you must do to bring about change. Thus, if your long-term objective is to become a lawyer, your short-term planning would entail obtaining your undergraduate degree, being admitted to law school, receiving your Juris Doctor, and passing the state bar exam.

> If your short-term goals are too high, you may give up too soon. If your long-term goals are too low, they may not give you enough enthusiasm to drive you over the bumps in the road along the way. (Darren LaCroix)

The importance of both short- and long-term goals cannot be overstated while planning plans. Together, these two will assist you in succeeding. Consider your long-term objectives as your destination and your short-term strategies as a route to getting there. Let's look at some advice on creating both long-term and short-term objectives with this in mind.

> When it is obvious that the goals cannot be reached, don't adjust the goals, adjust the action steps. (Confucius)

It may feel intimidating or overwhelming to set objectives, especially for the first time, but it doesn't have to be that way! Setting short- and long-term goals should be a creative and liberating process where you can express everything you have been thinking about for a while.

Remember that your results will be better if your aims are clearer and more sincere. Saying, for instance, "I want to make a lot of money" is too general to be very helpful. Search for something more doable as a replacement. A far more concrete and practical aim is, "I want to create my own business and, after three years, produce revenues of $250,000."

Once you've established clear long-term objectives, you may divide them into more manageable short-term objectives or stages you can take to carry them out.

Prepared to begin? Here are some pointers to get you started with your short- and long-term goal planning:

> Every goal that you will ever pursue will require a plan of action. Whether you are pursuing your life's destiny or striving to obtain a particular goal, you must be able to see things as you desire them to be. (T. D. Jakes)

Seek solitude.

Though it may seem obvious, it's crucial to set aside some quiet time for planning, brainstorming, and thinking. You can do this with a friend or a close person you trust. Find a location that suits you and allows you to immerse yourself fully. A park or coffee should be ideal. For taking notes, bring some paper and a pencil with you. You should begin the discussion, whether alone or with your ally, by asking open-ended questions and reflecting on where your life is now and where you want it to be. Be brutally honest and engage in in-depth brainstorming, but don't be afraid to put everything on the table. Once you have an idea of where you'd like to see yourself in a few years, you can start the short-term planning process for making it happen. Doing this repeatedly would be ideal to fully work out what it is that you want to do and how you're going to accomplish it realistically.

Make a list.

Make a long-term goal list of all the things you'd like to accomplish. Be sure to write everything down. Don't be alarmed at length; the point is to get everything down. Ask yourself questions like, What do you want to do? Where would you like to reside? How much money do you hope to earn? What do you want to accomplish? How would you like to feel? Asking yourself these questions would surely help you identify your short- and long-term goals.

> Set daily, monthly, and long-term goals and
> dreams. Don't ever be afraid to dream too big.
> Nothing is impossible. If you believe in yourself,
> you can achieve it. (Nastia Liukin)

Identify the objectives you hope to achieve.

Once you have everything written down, it's time to take a close look at your list of long-term objectives and decide which one, or maybe two or three, you would most like to accomplish. Which activities would make you the happiest? Which ones supersede the others? You may start breaking down the list's most significant or urgent concerns into manageable actions once you've determined which ones they are.

Break them up.

It's time to divide your objectives into more manageable steps. What is the short-term preparation necessary to accomplish your long-term objectives? Making a list of everything you require is a good idea if your objective is to launch a business. For example, this may entail researching, developing a strategy, sourcing your capital or finance, selecting and registering a business name, and obtaining necessary licenses and permissions. To ensure that your short-term personal objectives are completed, give each one a deadline and record them in your planner or calendar.

> Things that matter most must never be at the mercy of things that matter least. (Richard Koch)

Regularly assess goal progress.

Setting objectives and then evaluating them are entirely different things. Utilize technology, but be deliberate about concentrating on your objectives and goals. Make VIP appointments with yourself and give yourself reminders to assess your progress regularly. Look closely at what is and isn't occurring. As you see errors, fix them. Rewarding oneself is important when you attain goals.

Have a partner who is accountable.

It's important to have a partner to keep you motivated toward a goal. Long-term objectives may be accomplished with the assistance of an accountability partner who helps you stay on track. Owners may find inspiration and motivation to carry the objective by being aware of what they need, aligning, prioritizing, measuring, and having conversations about the procedure, processes, and support.

Keep the 80/20 rule.

Every leader requires a structure of accountability, such as a coach or partner, who ensures that the emphasis remains on what is long-term and vital rather than getting diverted by what is urgent. The 80/20 rule is a tried-and-true method for success. Recognize with clarity that 20 percent of your objectives and pursuits account for 80 percent of your output.

Tame your thoughts.

Your thoughts shape your reality. Every thought you have affects you in some manner, whether it's how you feel, do, or treat others. This could work against us or in our favor. Our thoughts can either motivate kindness and effect positive change or guide us down counterproductive or even dangerous avenues.

You may choose to think about living in the moment or making plans for the future. Your thoughts influence where you direct your energy and how it manifests in your life.

Thoughts are surely strong, but you are stronger than thoughts. Your thoughts are under your control.

Occasionally, it indeed looks like ideas just come to us out of nowhere, and certainly, that may happen. You influence that thinking even if it does. How will you use it? What is your reaction to it? Do you want to embrace that particular concept, or should you just let it go? You may design your thoughts to ensure that they are helpful and that you can balance your current activities with your plans by making these choices.

You may unleash your inner dragon and use that fierce creativity to change your life when you learn to regulate your thoughts. You can tell when your ideas in the present are harming your goals for the future and when your thoughts about the future are preventing you from experiencing your life to the fullest. Your thinking can be molded to become more rational. Your thoughts can "create happiness" for you.

It takes practice and fine-tuning to plan for the future while residing in the present. You'll need to become conscious of your inclinations and try to overcome them. You'll need to develop the ability to conceive thoughts that motivate you to take actions beneficial to your present and future self. And to connect the dots between the life you are presently experiencing and the life you want for the future, you'll need to learn how to draw backward.

When it comes to focusing, your history and your future are not mutually exclusive. Both of them are yours. Take ownership of both, live them both, and be happy while bringing about happiness.

Benefits of Living in the Now

The most important (and undervalued) skill in the world is the ability to focus on the present. The article from last week on keeping your thoughts quiet throughout the day was very popular, but it only hinted at the advantages.

A quiet trip to the store is just one benefit of the present habit. Even if you have no spiritual goals, there are countless everyday applications for cultivating mindfulness.

- *Cravings become more obvious and less difficult to resist.* To stop smoking, you must be aware of your cravings and find a different way to deal with them than by lighting up. That is the only objective, and it is modest enough to be reached at any time. If you lose sight of that, you can think that quitting is some enormous, impossibly lofty objective you must maintain for the rest of your life. With everything else, it functions the same.

- *It lessens the intensity of bodily pain.* It may be the last thing you expect, but focusing on the discomfort in your sore stomach or stubbed toe will make it much easier to handle. When you move away from a painful experience, it combines bitterness, wishful thinking, guilt, and other forms of mental neediness. This is what transforms suffering from agony. It's incredible how much the pain may be reduced when you focus solely on it.

- *Fear of large projects fades away.* You can't genuinely complete a project in its entirety for the same reason that you can't complete a workout. Every project consists of a single activity, the majority of which are no more complicated than picking up the phone, explaining something to someone, looking up someone's contact information online, or drawing up a model. Once you have a plan in place, moving forward is simple as long as you focus on the immediate needs and only zoom out to identify those needs.

- *You start acting more intelligently without even realizing it.* When I'm paying attention, I see that I'm more likely to hang up my jeans than to let them fall to the ground. Creating a life of clothing on the floor and one of relative order and respect for oneself needs almost the same amount of effort. An intuitive, in-the-moment feeling of what is prudent to do is one of the most pleasant effects of the mindfulness habit.

CHAPTER 10

Making Financial Goals for Your Future

Establishing your short- and medium- and long-term monetary objectives is essential to becoming financially independent. You may spend more than you should if you have yet to have any particular goals that you are working toward. You won't have enough money when you need it for unexpected costs, let alone when you wish to retire and start living off your savings. It's possible to get caught up in a never-ending cycle of credit card debt, leaving you with the feeling that you'll never have enough money to get properly insured and making you more exposed than you need to be to deal with some of the more significant threats that life presents.

As everyone discovered during the epidemic and continues to learn monthly, not even the most cautious individual can be prepared for every possible emergency. Thinking ahead allows you to consider the various potential outcomes of a situation and decide how best to organize yourself to deal with them. You should make this a continuous process to mold your life and ambitions to match the changes that will occur.

The annual financial planning process provides an opportunity to formally examine your objectives, bring them up to date, and assess your advancement from the previous year. If this is your first time doing so, now is the time to establish goals for yourself so that you can get on a solid financial footing or continue to do so. The following is a list of goals, ranging from short-term to long-term, that financial experts advocate creating to assist you in learning how to learn how to live comfortably within your means, reduce the number of money problems you experience, and save money for retirement.

Financial Objectives for the Short Term

Regarding your finances, establishing objectives for the short term can provide you with the foundation and the confidence boost you need to attain the longer-term, more ambitious goals. These initial steps can be accomplished with relatively minimal effort in as little as a year: Make a plan for your money and stick to it. Create a fund for unexpected expenses. Reduce the amount of credit card debt preventing you from moving forward.

Create a spending plan.

Knowing where you are heading is only possible once you have a solid understanding of where you are now. You may be surprised to see how much money is lost each month due to various oversights.

Utilizing a free budgeting application such as Mint is a simple and efficient method for keeping track of your spending habits. It will compile the information from each of your accounts into a centralized location, allowing you to categorize each purchase into the appropriate category. You can also make a budget the old-fashioned way by reading through your bank statements and bills from the past few months and classifying each purchase using a spreadsheet or on paper. This would be another way to establish a budget.

It's possible that if you order Seamless for lunch every day that you work from home (or spend that much on lunches with coworkers if you're back in an office), it will cost you $315 for the month, which comes out to $15 per meal for twenty-one workdays. You may discover that you are spending an additional $100 every weekend on date-night meals with your significant other. When you are aware of how you are spending your money and when you let that knowledge lead you, you will be able to arrive at more informed conclusions regarding the future destination of your financial resources. Do you feel the pleasure and convenience of eating out at restaurants are worth $315 each month? If that's the case, that's fantastic—just make sure you can pay for it. If so, you've just learned an easy strategy to save money each month that you can implement immediately. You can either look for ways to reduce the money you spend when you eat out, substitute some meals from restaurants or takeaway with ones you prepare at home, or combine the two approaches.

Establish a savings account.

A reserve for unforeseen costs is what's known as an emergency fund, and it's money that's been set aside particularly for that purpose. To get started, a goal of between $500 and $1,000 is a decent starting point. When you reach that objective, you will want to increase it so that your emergency fund can handle more significant financial challenges, such as being laid off from your job. If you did not have an emergency fund before the COVID-19 epidemic, you probably wished you had one now that it is here. And even if you did have one, it may have been depleted, and you now need to work on building it back up.

Save at least three months' worth of expenses to cover your financial obligations and basic needs. However, I recommend saving six months' worth of costs. This is essential advice if you are married and work for the same company as your spouse or in an area with limited job prospects. I recommend identifying at least one area of your spending that can be reduced to assist in funding your emergency funds.

You can also use an online financial services company that provides consumer debt settlement, mortgage shopping, and personal loans. Decluttering and organizing one's home is another way to build an emergency savings fund. You can generate additional cash by selling things you no longer require on online marketplaces like eBay or Craigslist or hosting a yard sale. Consider turning it into a part-time job so that you can put the money you make toward savings.

You can also register a savings account and then set up an automatic transfer for the amount you have calculated. You can save each month (by utilizing your budget) up until the point where you have reached your target for your emergency fund. "If you get a bonus, a tax refund, or even an 'extra' monthly salary—which happens two months out of the year if you are paid biweekly—save that money as soon as it enters your bank account. If you wait until the end of the month to move that money, there is a good chance that you will wind up spending it rather than putting it away for the future," she advises.

Although you have other financial objectives, such as retirement savings, putting together an emergency fund is your top priority. The financial security that will allow you to accomplish the rest of your objectives will be generated through your savings account.

Make payments on your credit cards.

There is an argument among financial experts on which should come first: building an emergency fund or paying off credit card debt. Some people believe that you should start an emergency fund even if you already have credit card debt since, if you don't have one, every unanticipated expense will put you in a deeper hole with your credit card debt. It's better to be safe than sorry. Some people believe you should focus on paying off your credit card debt first because the interest is so expensive and will make it much more difficult for you to achieve any other financial objective. Choose the worldview that resonates with you the most, or combine elements of both into your everyday life for a more well-rounded outlook.

When it comes to paying off credit card debt, I suggest making a list of all your bills in order of interest rate, going from lowest to highest, and then making only the minimum payment on all your debts other than the one with the highest interest rate. Use any funds available to make additional payments on the card with the highest interest rate.

The approach that I suggest is known as the debt avalanche method. One further strategy to take into consideration is known as the debt snowball. You pay off your bills using the snowball technique in the sequence of smallest to largest, regardless of the interest rate associated with each debt. The rationale behind this approach is that if you pay off your smallest obligation first, you will feel a sense of satisfaction that will motivate you to pay off your next-smallest loan and so on, until you have paid off all your debts and are debt-free.

Persons with $10,000 or more in unsecured debt (such as credit card debt) who cannot afford the statutory minimum payments may want to consider debt negotiation or settlement as an alternative. The Federal Trade Commission regulates the businesses that provide these services. In exchange for a fee, typically a percentage of the total debt or a percentage of the amount of debt reduction, which the consumer should only pay after a successful negotiation, these businesses work on the consumer's behalf to reduce the debt by as much as 50 percent.

This method can help consumers eliminate their debt in two to four years. Debt settlement can have a negative impact on your credit score, and creditors have the right to pursue legal action against consumers for unpaid payments.

Midterm financial goals.

It is time to start working toward your midterm financial goals once you have established a budget, created an emergency fund, and paid off your credit card debt—or at least made a good dent in those three short-term goals. Once you have accomplished these, it is time to work toward your long-term financial goals. Your short-term and long-term financial objectives will be connected through the completion of these tasks.

Purchase both life insurance and insurance against income loss due to disability.

Do you have a wife or children who rely on you for financial support? If this is the case, you should get life insurance so that your loved ones will be taken care of in the event of your untimely death. The majority of people's insurance requirements may be satisfied by getting life insurance, which is both the simplest and the most affordable type of life insurance. Working with an insurance broker may assist you in obtaining the best deal possible on a policy. Medical underwriting is required for the majority of term life insurance policies, but unless you have a significant illness, you should be able to locate at least one insurance provider who is willing to sell you a policy.

Additionally, I recommend that you purchase disability insurance to safeguard your income in the event that you are unable to work. The majority of firms offer this coverage to their employees. In the event that they do not, folks have the ability to get it on their own up until the age of retirement.

If you suffer from a serious illness or injury that prevents you from working due to its severity, disability insurance can help replace a portion of your lost income. You (and your family, if you have one) may be able to live more comfortably than you would be able to. This is yet another reason why it is essential to have some money set aside in case of an emergency.

Repay your outstanding student loans.

Student debt puts a significant strain on the monthly finances of a lot of people. If you are able to reduce or eliminate such payments, you will have more disposable income, which will make it simpler for you to save money for retirement and achieve your other objectives. Refinancing your existing student debt into a new loan with a lower interest rate is one approach that can assist you in paying off your existing debt. Be aware, however, that if you refinance your federal student loans with a private lender, you run the risk of losing some of the benefits that come with federal student loans. These benefits include income-based repayment, deferment, and forbearance, all of which can be of assistance if you run into financial difficulties.

If, for instance, you began your retirement with a portfolio worth $1 million, took out $40,000 in the first year (which is 4 percent of $1 million), and then increased your withdrawal by the rate of inflation each year thereafter ($40,000 plus 2 percent in the second year, which is $40,800; $40,800 plus 2 percent in the third year, which is $41,616, and so on), you would have had enough money to last your entire thirty-year retirement without having to worry about running out of money. This is the reason why you commonly read 4 percent as a rule of thumb when considering retirement.

In most cases, you actually end up with more money at the end of thirty years at 4 percent, but in the worst-case scenario, you would have run out of money in the year 30 if you used that interest rate. The only word of caution I would offer in this regard is that simply because 4 percent has prevailed in every scenario throughout history does not ensure that it will continue to do so in the years to come.

Boost your savings for retirement.

For the majority of people who have a retirement plan sponsored by their company, the employer will match a percentage of what they are paid. They may contribute an additional 3 percent or even 7 percent of your gross compensation. If you contribute enough to your retirement account to receive the full matching contribution from your company, not only will you get a return on your investment of 100 percent but you will also have taken the most significant step toward funding your retirement.

What hurts me is that people do not put money into their retirement plan because either they can't afford it or they are afraid of the stock market.

I recommend making contributions to an IRA at the beginning of the year rather than at the end when most people tend to do it so that the money has more time to grow and so that you have a larger amount with which to retire. Most people tend to make these contributions at the end of the year.

Sitting at your desk with a looming deadline while your mind is elsewhere is a situation that we all have experienced at some point. Things are not moving forward, although you have been doing your hardest. You must keep your attention on the work currently in front of you. You have the drive to get it done. But you just can't concentrate.

In this digital age, it is easy for us to become distracted. The necessity to manage ever-increasing amounts of information in various formats has become increasingly pressing due to the widespread availability of information. Both our time and our attention are wasted by it.

One of the ills of our time is the inability to focus on the activity that is now taking place; thus, everyone is interested in learning how to focus better and concentrate. Despite this, it is a problem that should be addressed because there are benefits to be gained from improved concentration and focus.

What Does Concentration Mean?

According to what Remez Sasson mentioned in *Willpower and Self-Discipline*, focus is the capability of directing one's attention by one's own will. To concentrate is to exercise control over one's attention. It is the ability to focus on a single topic, object, or thought while simultaneously blocking out of one's consciousness any other thoughts, ideas, feelings, and sensations irrelevant to the issue.

This final step is when the majority of us run into problems. Concentrating means shutting off or ignoring other thoughts, ideas, feelings, or sensations that are not directly relevant to the task. It is crucial not to pay attention to the numbers, beeps, and other indicators that we have a new message, a new update, a new "like," or a new follower!

Using our mobile phones and computers takes up most of our time during a typical day. The likes of WhatsApp, email, Telegram, and the other half-dozen applications that are important to our work all provide us with a steady stream of communications at all times. We are always looking for new information that will assist us in finding solutions to the challenges we face daily or in completing our work.

Productivity suffers whenever there are frequent interruptions. It will take more time to complete the assignment. We need to become more attentive listeners. Whether with our partners or coworkers, we need to comprehend things better, which leads to misunderstanding, misinterpretation, and conflict. Memory is impacted as a result. Because of our poor memory or inability to retrieve knowledge quickly, our personal lives and professional images suffer as a result.

A Look at the Factors That Influence Our Concentration

On certain days, it feels as though our ability to concentrate is being challenged from every angle. The focus is influenced not only by internal elements but also by external or environmental factors. It is helpful if you want to learn how to increase your focus and memory to understand what is currently getting in the way of those improvements.

Distraction

While we are in the middle of doing anything, we are inundated with a never-ending stream of information, some brand new and some somewhat dated. Researchers have discovered that our brains are so conditioned for this type of distraction that the mere sight of our smartphones is enough to hamper our ability to focus. We continually evaluate the information to determine whether it is meaningful, sufficient, or meaningless. The sheer volume that is coming in makes it difficult to decide whether we require further information to make decisions.

Insufficient sleep

Researchers have discovered that not getting enough sleep may result in decreased attentiveness, slower mental processes, and reduced attention. You will have a more challenging time focusing your attention, and there is a chance that you will need clarification. Consequently, your capacity to carry out some jobs, particularly those that involve reasoning or logic, may need to be improved. Your ability to concentrate and remember things is negatively impacted even further by chronic sleep deprivation. Suppose you need to focus on something other than the task at hand. In that case, it is highly improbable that the information will be stored in either your short-term or long-term memory, according to research by Dr. Allison T. Siebern of the Sleep Medicine Center at Stanford University.

Insufficient amount of action in the physical realm

Have you ever noticed how strenuous physical activity makes you feel calmer and more energized throughout the day? Your muscles are more likely to become contracted when you don't get enough exercise. You may be experiencing tightness in your neck, shoulders, and chest, and this ongoing, low-level discomfort may make it difficult for you to concentrate.

Eating habits

What we put into our bodies, especially the food we consume, plays a role in how we feel, including how sharp and clear our minds are throughout the day. Memory loss, weariness, and an inability to concentrate are some side effects that can occur when our brains aren't getting the nutrition they need to function correctly. Because the brain needs specific critical fatty acids, low-fat diets may make concentrating difficult. Other restrictive diets may have a detrimental effect on concentration either by failing to supply the necessary nutrients for the brain or by causing feelings of hunger, cravings, or unwellness in the body, all of which are in and of themselves distracting.

Environment

The surroundings may hinder your concentration, but this depends on the task. A noise level that is too high is a problem, yet a significant number of people also struggle to concentrate when it is too quiet. The high-energy, nameless hum of a coffee shop may inspire focus, but the overheard chat of two coworkers may distract it. What counts is not simply the overall noise level but the sort of noise that is present. While it may be easier for less distinguishable instrumentals to keep you attentive to the activity, singing along to a favorite song is sure to divert your attention rapidly. Your vision may be negatively impacted by either too bright or too faint lighting. It is uncomfortable to be in an environment that is either too hot or too cold.

Your ability to concentrate may suffer if any of these factors are present. The good news is that each one of them can be solved.

Conditions about the Act of Concentrating

You may be having cognitive issues, physical issues, psychological issues, issues related to your lifestyle, or environmental issues if you frequently find that you are unable to focus your thoughts and if these difficulties persist. You may need to momentarily accept that your focus is low and learn a few tactics to decrease the impact, or you may just need to know to take the dips in concentration as they occur. This will depend on the cause. If you have trouble concentrating and believe your challenges go beyond the listed items, you should talk to a trained specialist.

Conditions of a more general kind that could apply include the following:

- *Cognitive.* If you find that you forget things quickly, this could signify your focus is suffering. Your memory only sometimes serves you well, as evidenced by the fact that you frequently misplace items and need help recalling events that took place only recently. Suppose you notice that your mind is busy and always thinking of many things owing to concerns or important events. In that case, this is another sign that your ability to concentrate is negatively affected intellectually. It is impossible to focus effectively when unwanted ideas and problems keep popping into your head and demanding your attention.
- *Psychological.* It is challenging to concentrate when you are experiencing symptoms of depression and are feeling down

in the dumps. You may have trouble focusing on a single job when you are grieving the death of a loved one, which is known as grief, or when you are experiencing anxiety. Both of these states can make it challenging to deal with loss.

- *Medical.* Various health disorders, including diabetes, hormonal abnormalities, and a low red blood cell count, can cause concentration problems. Some medications not only make you feel sleepy or foggy but also severely damage your ability to concentrate.

- *Environment.* Working conditions, shared spaces, and intense or unpleasant work dynamics can all lead to a lack of attention. Other factors that may contribute include poor working conditions. When we are emotionally spent as a result of burnout, stress brought on by either our personal or professional lives or both, it can be challenging for us to focus our attention. Similarly, our surroundings can make our bodies uncomfortable by producing impacts that we are conscious of (such as heat, light, and noise) and others that don't completely register with us (tension, negativity, monitoring).

- *Lifestyle.* Lack of concentration can be caused by fatigue, hunger, and dehydration. Memory problems and difficulties concentrating and focusing may be caused by living habits that involve skipping too many meals, eating a diet high in saturated fat, or drinking excessive alcohol.

Methods for Enhancing Your Ability to Focus and Concentrate

You should now understand why you need assistance with your concentration. How can you improve your ability to concentrate? The question of how to improve focus cannot be answered definitively, but the following suggestions may be of assistance.

- *Eliminate distractions.*

  How can we improve our ability to focus when we are constantly inundated with information? It should become routine for you to schedule time to complete a particular endeavor or activity. During this time, you should request to be left alone or go to a place where other people are not likely to disturb you, such as a library, a coffee shop, or a room.

  You should log out of social media and other apps, turn off notifications, and conceal your phone in a bag or backpack so it can't be seen. According to what was published in HBR, researchers discovered that cognitive capacity was significantly improved when the phone was switched off and hidden from view. Finishing what you need to do should be your primary emphasis. Concentration can be improved by blocking distractions, whether from within or without.

- *Take on fewer tasks at once.*

  When we challenge ourselves to juggle numerous tasks, we feel accomplished. It's a recipe for less attention, less concentration, and less productivity. And decreased productivity has been linked to feelings of exhaustion. You can listen to a podcast while simultaneously responding to an email, or you can talk to someone over the phone while simultaneously preparing a report. These are both examples of multitasking. This kind of multitasking makes it difficult for you to concentrate, which in turn lowers the quality of your job.

- *Meditation and mindful awareness practice are encouraged.*

  It can boost well-being and mental fitness and improve focus by meditating or engaging in other mindfulness activities. Meditating brings a gradual quieting of the mind and a general loosening of all body muscles. During the process, we focus on our breath to keep our minds from wandering off and distracting us. We can, with enough experience, learn to use our breath to bring our attention back to a specific job so that we can complete it successfully, even if we are stopped while we are working on it.

- *Get more sleep.*

    Several things can disrupt your sleep. One of the most typical activities that people engage in immediately before going to bed is reading on an electronic device, such as a computer, phone, or tablet, or viewing their preferred movie or television show on an LED television. According to the findings of many pieces of research, these types of devices emit predominantly blue light. This kind of light will excite the retina in your eye and hinder the secretion of melatonin, a hormone that encourages the brain to get ready for sleep. Use "blue light" glasses or a filter to reduce the amount of blue light that enters your eyes, or avoid using any electronic devices before going to bed. Other methods to improve sleep include avoiding exertion in the late afternoon or evening, staying hydrated throughout the day, using journaling or breathing exercises to quiet the mind, and developing a pattern and plan for going to bed that is consistent and routine.

- *You can decide to concentrate on the present.*

    It may seem contradictory when you're having trouble concentrating but remember that you have control over where your attention goes. Concentration is difficult to achieve when one's thoughts constantly wander back to the past or forward to the unknown. Make an effort to move on from the things that have happened in the past, even if it won't be easy. Acknowledge the impact, how it made you feel, and what you took away from it, and then let go of those things.

    Similarly, notice your worries about the future, pay attention to where in your body you feel the concern, and then make the conscious decision to let it go. Our goal is to teach our mental resources to concentrate on the particulars of what is essential at present. Our thoughts travel in the path that we give our attention to.

- *Take a quick break and regroup.*

  When you focus on something for an extended period, your ability to maintain that focus may begin to deteriorate. This may also be contrary to common sense. You may need help focusing more on the activity at hand.

  According to several studies, our brains overlook sources of constant stimulus. After that, taking very brief breaks in which you divert your attention to anything else may significantly increase your ability to concentrate mentally. When you find yourself becoming stuck when working on a project the next time, make sure to give yourself a break. Move about, engage in conversation with another person, or even transfer to a different activity. You are going to return with a clearer head, which will allow you to maintain your previous level of performance.

- *Reconnect with the natural world.*

  According to research on the topic, simply having plants in an office space can aid in improving concentration and productivity and overall workplace satisfaction and air purity. Your ability to concentrate and sense of well-being can be enhanced by making time to stroll in a nearby park or to stop and smell the roses or other flowers in your yard.

- *Educate your mental faculties.*

  According to preliminary findings from scientific research, adults who participate in brain training exercises have been shown to improve their cognitive capacities, particularly their capacity to concentrate. Playing these kinds of games with your brain can also help you improve your working memory and short-term memory, as well as your processing speed and your ability to solve problems. Jigsaw puzzles, sudoku, chess, and various types of mentally challenging video games are a few examples of this category of games.

- *Exercise.*

  You should move your body first thing in the morning by performing simple exercises. According to an article published in the May 2013 issue of the *Harvard Men's Health Watch*, consistent physical activity causes the production of neurotransmitters that are essential for memory, focus, and mental acuity. Dopamine, norepinephrine, and serotonin are all neurotransmitters that can be increased by exercise; these will affect one's ability to concentrate and pay attention. Compared to individuals in poor physical health, those who participate in some type of physical activity, such as exercise or sports, have superior cognitive performance. Moving around helps to loosen up the muscles and release tension that has built up in the body. Your state of mind will improve along with the state of your body because of the strong connection between the two.

- *Take in some musical sounds.*

  Research has demonstrated that listening to music may have a therapeutic effect on our brains. Some types of music can make it easier to concentrate, while other types of music may be a distraction. When it comes to focusing, most experts think that classical music and the sounds of nature, such as water running, are the best options, whereas music with lyrics and human voices may be too distracting. There are a variety of apps and services that provide background music and soundscapes that are tailored to different types of concentration and work requirements.

- *Eat healthfully.*

  Choose foods that will keep your energy up, keep your blood sugar in check, and fuel your brain. Fruits, vegetables, and foods high in fiber are all excellent ways to maintain a healthy blood sugar level. Reduce your consumption of sugary foods and drinks because these can cause spikes and dips in your blood sugar levels, leaving you light-headed or sleepy.

- *For it to function correctly, your brain requires a substantial amount of healthy fat.*

  Nuts, berries, avocados, and coconut oil are all excellent ways to add healthy fats to your diet, which can help your brain operate more efficiently. Research has shown that certain foods such as blueberries can boost concentration and memory for up to five hours after consumption. This is due to an enzyme that stimulates the flow of oxygen and blood to the brain, which helps with memory and our ability to focus and learn new information. Blueberries are just one example of these types of foods. Potassium is found in leafy green foods like spinach and others leafy greens. Potassium helps speed up the connections between neurons in our brain, which can make our brain more responsive.

- *Establish a daily focus of attention.*

  You should write out what you want to do each day, preferably the night before, and choose a single priority that you will work hard to complete. This will assist in focusing your thoughts on what is essential, allowing you to tackle the more significant tasks first and save the less important concerns for a later time. You can avoid feeling overwhelmed by tackling enormous chores by breaking them down into smaller chunks. Finding true priorities can assist in relieving distracting anxiety and accomplishing even modest daily goals can help wire your brain for future success.

- *Make room for work to be done.*

  You should design a quiet room specifically for working. Desk organizers, noise-canceling headphones, an adjustable monitor, and adjustable lighting can all be help-ful additions to an office, but not everyone can afford a well-appointed workspace. You should get rid of any clutter in plain sight, ensure that the area is as ergonomic and pleasant as you can make it, and work to keep it clean and well-ventilated.

- *Put a timer to use.*

    Utilizing a timer or the alarm on your phone will help you train your brain to concentrate extremely hard on a specific subject. Determine the activity that you intend to carry out first. Concentrate on the task at hand while the timer is set for twenty minutes (in most cases, the maximum allowed is thirty minutes). Whenever the alarm goes off, stop what you're doing and relax for five minutes. You have two options: one is to restart the timer, and the other is to go for a short stroll while performing some stretching exercises. This method has been demonstrated to be beneficial in enhancing one's level of concentration.

- *Alter your focus.*

    Even if we desire to focus on a specific activity, there are instances when we cannot make progress, and our minds require a new topic to concentrate on. Try switching to other tasks or doing something you enjoy doing instead. Alternating between different kinds of work helps keep you attentive and productive for an extended period of time.

    It won't happen immediately, but you can learn to enhance your attention by practicing it often. It takes professional athletes, like golfers, sprinters, and gymnasts, a significant amount of time to practice (and they almost always have a coach) to achieve their full potential and focus on making the right move at the proper time.

    The first thing you need to do to improve your concentration is to become aware of its impact on your life. If you are having trouble keeping your commitments, are frequently distracted by things that are not important, or are not making progress toward your goals, it is time to get assistance with your concentration so that you can concentrate on the things that are most important to you.

Learning to focus while on the job is a skill that will serve you well throughout your life and career. You'll find that you can accomplish more important things and feel better about yourself as a result of improving your concentration. Living a meaningful and gratifying life requires more than just getting things done; it also requires creating room in your schedule for things that bring you joy and satisfaction.

Chapter 11

Habits That Can Lead to Success in the Moment

Aside from the chance factor, a significant portion of what contributes to the achievements of some individuals is the development of particular patterns of behavior. It is beneficial to gain an understanding of what these habits are and how to implement them in one's own life.

In light of this, I've compiled a list of the ten behaviors that successful people consistently exhibit.

Organization

Organization is one of the traits of successful people that are highlighted most frequently in interviews with other successful people. This sort of organization requires planning as well as the establishment of priorities and objectives.

Before retiring for the night, Joel Brown, the man behind the website Addicted2Success.com, recommends making a prioritized to-do list to get ready for the following day.

According to Jack Dorsey, who is no longer employed by Twitter but was one of the company's cofounders, Sunday is a significant day for organizations to "getting ready for the remainder of the week."

Unwinding and decompressing

It is noteworthy to notice that one of the most frequently reported characteristics of successful people is the tendency to relax, either via the practice of meditation or simply by avoiding distractions.

Those who are well-organized naturally have a more straightforward time unwinding. As a result, it's possible that relaxation is more of a natural consequence than a deliberate choice for some people.

It's also possible that a successful person uses the "taking a breath" process to prepare themselves for the exertion that lies ahead mentally. Concentrating on one's breathing for three to five minutes at the beginning of an effort to achieve a meditative or calm state is one of the first things that should be done.

Taking action

The third entry on the list of successful individuals' behaviors is the habit of always taking action. Even if it is necessary to prioritize, organize, and plan, a plan will only be potential if it is followed by actual execution.

People who are successful act rapidly and frequently. In addition, even though it may appear paradoxical, James Clear claims that people act (start anyway) before they feel ready.

Successful people are those who, when others are coming up with excuses not to act, are the ones who go ahead and take that initial step, even if it sounds ridiculous.

Hygiene and personal care

The fourth habit on the list of successful people's routines is to take care of themselves in terms of their nutrition, exercise routine, and cleanliness.

Some people find that proper self-care necessitates adhering to arduous routines and leading highly disciplined lives. However, this is different for others. When asked about the routine that has had the most significant beneficial impact on his life, Elon Musk, CEO of Tesla Motors, answered clearly by saying that he meditates daily. Showering was all that Musk had to say about it.

Positive attitude

Many people who have achieved great success believe that a positive attitude is not just one factor that contributes to success but also one of the sources of success itself.

According to Joel Brown, highly successful people make feelings of appreciation and positive self-talk a priority in their life. In addition, according to Brown, merely having a cheerful mindset and expressing thankfulness is not enough. To have an even fuller sensation, you should also consider the reasons behind your gratitude.

Networking

Successful people understand the importance of exchanging ideas with others through the process of networking. They are also aware of the importance of working together and in teams, typical outcomes when one networks.

According to author Thomas Corley, successful people know how important it is to surround themselves with other successful people. According to Corley, 79 percent of wealthy people spend at least five hours each month engaging in networking activities.

Frugality

Being thrifty is not the same thing as being cheap. The practice of being frugal with one's resources and one's finances is known as frugality. Being frugal is another characteristic of this way of life. Avoiding unnecessary expenditures is the first step toward developing frugal habits, which inevitably leads to increased productivity.

Successful people don't blow their budgets. They opt to look around and be flexible with their prices instead. The straightforward action of saving more money than one spends ultimately leads to financial prosperity.

Getting up very early

The more time an individual can invest in becoming successful, the higher the likelihood that the individual will achieve that accomplishment. Early rising is a common practice among those who are successful in life, and it is a frequent tendency among those who are successful.

The Early Riser's Club comprises many successful people, but some members stand out more than others. Among them is Sir Richard Branson, CEO of Virgin Group; Robert Iger, CEO of Disney; and Marissa Mayer, former CEO of Yahoo!

Sharing

Successful people make it a habit to give back to their communities, whether it's through financial contributions to charities or the exchange of ideas. They are aware of the importance of generosity, and most think that the fruits of their achievement should be something other than acquiring wealth for themselves.

Bill Gates, Oprah Winfrey, and Mark Zuckerberg are just a few examples of the most famous and successful philanthropists in modern history.

When it comes to giving and receiving, a person's level of money is not necessarily a relevant consideration. Volunteering in your community or at a school in your area does not cost anything, but doing so could provide assistance in areas where it is most required.

Reading

It's essential to remember that successful people are avid readers. Most people read to acquire knowledge or gain perspective, while some also read for enjoyment.

The successful entrepreneur Mark Cuban typically spends more than three hours per day reading. In his book *How to Win at the Sport of Business: If I Can Do It, You Can Do It*, he claimed, "If I can do it, you can do it. To this day, I believe that if I put in enough time to consume all of the material, particularly now that the Internet makes it so readily accessible, I can have an advantage in any technology business."

Many people scratch their heads and wonder what they can do to succeed. Still, they need to realize that they already have everything they need to succeed on the level they've imagined for themselves.

The habits they've developed over time have allowed them to become where they are today. People's actions are determined by their practices 95 percent of the time.

The quality of the habits you create will decide not just who you are today but also all you have accomplished and will achieve in the future.

You, too, have the potential to achieve success and have a happy, prosperous life if you commit to developing healthy behaviors and wholesome routines.

The concept of success in human life has been analyzed by some of history's most eminent intellectuals and philosophers for thousands of years. More than three decades of my life have been devoted to learning about this topic. I have discovered that the very finest people have built good habits throughout their lives.

To achieve your full potential in any endeavor, you must cultivate the seven valuable habits I will share.

- *They focus on achieving their goals.*

    Becoming goal-oriented should be the first habit you form.

    You need to develop the practice of setting objectives regularly and commit yourself to work from written goals that are both specific and attainable every day of your life. Everyone who has achieved great success has a strong focus on their goals. They are evident about what it is that they want. They have it written down, they have documented plans to get it, and as part of their daily routine, they go over their plans and work on implementing them.

You should educate yourself on the 80/20 rule to accomplish your objectives more effectively.

- *They are dedicated to achieving results.*

     Being motivated by the results of one's efforts is the second trait of highly successful people.

     This is a combination of two different procedures: The first is constantly enhancing one's knowledge and skills to become more proficient in one's work. The second strategy is one of managing one's time effectively. This entails establishing clear priorities for what you do and, afterward, focusing your undivided attention on the activity that best uses your time.

     Every truly successful person is highly focused on the results they achieve.

- *They are focused on taking action.*

     Taking action consistently is the third essential pattern of behavior that you need to cultivate.

     This is the practice that is necessary for achieving monetary success. It is the capacity to get on with the task at hand and complete it promptly. You can construct and continue to nurture a sense of urgency and a bias toward action. Maintaining a quick pace in all you do is necessary for your success.

     You must overcome your tendency to put things off till later, get over your worries, and dive headfirst into working toward accomplishing your most essential goals. The alignment of one's priorities with one's goals, results, and actions will, on their own, guarantee one's achievement of tremendous success.

     It is highly recommended that you learn how to use the SMART objectives I mentioned earlier to identify attainable aims that you can monitor and keep an eye on.

- *They have a focus on individuals and groups.*

  People orientation is the fourth habit that you need to develop.

  Relationships should take precedence over everything else in your life at this point. You have chosen to develop patience, kindness, compassion, and understanding within yourself. This decision is entirely up to you. Your capacity to get along well with others will determine a significant portion of your satisfaction throughout your life.

  The encouraging news is that when you decide to, you may transform into a lovely human being in your interactions with other people.

  According to Aristotle, the only way to successfully learn and maintain a habit is to engage in that practice consistently. You will internalize the attributes of a truly exceptional person and become that person the more you practice becoming that person in your connections with others and the more you put those qualities into practice.

  An excellent strategy to develop a lifestyle of positive thinking is to make an effort to be more agreeable with the people you interact with daily.

- *They take consideration of their health.*

  A health-conscious mindset is the fifth pattern of behavior that highly successful people cultivate.

  This indicates that you must monitor your diet carefully and always consume the proper meals appropriately. To keep your body flexible and in good shape, you must engage in regular physical activity and ensure every muscle and joint gets used. And last but not least, you need to cultivate appropriate patterns of rest and recreation that, in conjunction with a nutritious diet and regular physical activity, will allow you to enjoy a long and healthy life.

  Remember that your health is the most important thing you possess and that it is entirely subjected to the habits you create concerning how you choose to conduct your life.

- *They are honest.*

    Being honest and having integrity is the sixth habit to develop.

    In the final analysis, the person you become due to the experiences you have throughout your life is far more important than almost everything else.

    To be honest is to conduct all of one's activities under the "reality principle." You can see yourself and the world around you with total objectivity. You have very distinct standards that you hold yourself to, and you order your life according to those standards. You first create a vision for yourself, and then you proceed to live your life following the highest standards that you have for yourself. You never let anyone or anything cause you to violate your integrity or disturb your mental stability.

    This honesty of spirit is vital for taking pleasure in all the other positive habits you are working to cultivate.

- *They have a strong sense of self-control.*

    Self-discipline is the seventh habit, and it is the one habit that ensures success in developing all the other habits.

    The capacity to exercise self-discipline, self-mastery, and self-control is the single most significant attribute you can cultivate in yourself. Yet it is also one of the most difficult to achieve. Self-discipline is one of the most critical factors in determining one's level of achievement in life.

    Check out some of these motivational success quotes if you could use some assistance in maintaining your drive while working toward creating the life of your dreams.

    Every one of these behaviors, including focusing on goals, being driven by outcomes, focusing on actions, focusing on people, being health conscious, being honest, and having self-discipline, can be learned. Because of your routines, you have arrived where you are and become who you are. Since you were an infant, most of your behaviors have developed in an unintentional manner, even if you may not have realized it at the time.

Suppose you decide right now to find the definition of the habits that will lead you to great success. In that case, you can take complete control over shaping your character and personality and everything that will happen to you in the future. You can do this by finding the habits that will lead you to great success.

And when you cultivate the same positive behaviors that other successful individuals share, you will have the satisfaction of having success in common with those people. Your future will open up to limitless possibilities.

CHAPTER 12

Conclusion

While this book is not exhaustive and even as it tries to cover important concepts that help you become the real you both in the present and the future, it always takes practical approaches in each of its suggestions. The importance of living in the moment while being conscious about the future lies in finding purpose, truly living life, and realizing that we each only have a limited number of days on this earth. You have to enjoy every moment if you want to survive the eternity of life. Each day that follows has to be lived distinctly from the previous one and the one to come. Just as an atom is made of smaller indivisible particles and amino acids, the building blocks of proteins, the future is made up of nows. It is composed of the present little moments. They may be insignificant if you neglect them, but I genuinely tell you if you consciously strive to acknowledge them. You would realize that as little drops of water make a mighty ocean, your present moments can make your future the desired one.

As you realize that both your past and future depend on today, you will soon understand that as you live, you must evolve mentally, spiritually, and emotionally. The secret to evolving is being aware of your present moment. It not only affects your mental well-being but it does also help to keep you in both spiritual and emotional balance. You shouldn't live your life weighed or perturbed by any problems or limitations you might face. Instead, let your dream for the future be your driving force. Let it be the energy that spurs you forward. End each day ensuring you conquered the battle it brought to you so that tomorrow, if it doesn't bring new challenges, you can be rest assured to bask in the victories you have won from the previous day. That is how a perfect and desired future is created and earned.

Never allow your mind to be too preoccupied with the thoughts of the future that you forget to salvage the happiness and all the sweetness the present moment offers you. It is worth remembering that the present moment is the only time you can control the past and not the future. You can't control those, but you can control the moment. Mastering and dictating each moment would surely set your mind at rest as your unconscious mind registers it as a norm. It will significantly marvel how it stops thinking and wasting time and energy pondering the future's uncertainties. Make an effort to pay attention to the little things happening around you and fully appreciate the present. This does not need you to observe everything that is going on in your immediate environment. However, if you try to pay more attention to your regular activities, you can discover that they are much more intriguing than you initially imagined. As you are traveling to work, take note of the sunrise. Feel the chilly wind on your face when you go for a walk in the evening. This brings a feeling of peace and serenity. It helps relieve you of stress from the day's work.

Starting from the first question in the first chapter in part 1 of this book, you should have found a deep insight into knowing who you are, defining who you are in terms of your environment and the people you surround yourself with, by experiencing yourself and your environment. You would have learned how such things as insecurities and low self-esteem can distort the picture of your true self and hamper growth and development while blurring the bigger picture, the *future*, by making you constantly dwell on the very moments. By following through with the guide in dealing with insecurities, you will soon realize how easy it is to live in the moment and the freedom it bears. Avoiding being influenced by how people see you or how they want you to act toward them is another critical virtue you should develop. You must learn that successful people are always obsessed with the passion for attaining their goals, and many would detest you for this. It is okay, but trust me, only a few who see reason with you will stay by your side, and they matter. These are the people you should often associate with because there will come a time when you will need words of encouragement. They are suitable for this purpose. Avoid people who mistake your confidence for arrogance, who see your obsession as insanity, and overall, who do not believe in your dreams.

Remember, give it your all, use the mirror to shape who you want to be, utilize the power in the moments, always stay focused, develop SMART goals that serve as a guide, and never forget to reward yourself for each successful milestone you conquer.

About the Author

Dr. Miguel A. Fernandez was born in New York but is currently in private practice just north of Boston, Massachusetts. He lives there with his wife and two daughters. He is a doctor of chiropractic. His specialty is sports medicine, and he is certified by the *International Federation of Sports Chiropractic.* He has also competed in various combat-type sports, including judo and tae kwon do, in which he holds multiple martial arts belts. His hobbies include reading, writing, collaborating to create books people would love to read, and contemplating ways to help people. His favorite pastime is running and playing with his youngest child, and a close second is joking and laughing with his oldest child.

If you would like to join the author's mailing list, send the words "Add me" to drmiguel.fernandez@gmail.com.